WORKING FOR LEEK

recollections of life working in Leek's textile trades

edited by
Paul Anderton

based on interviews conducted by
Paul Anderton, Joan Bennett, Rowena Lovatt,
Trevor Siggers, Cathryn Walton.

Published jointly by
Leek and Moorlands Historical Trust
Leek and District Historical Society
2006

ISBN 0-9544080-9-8

Three Counties Publishing (Books) Ltd

Acknowledgements

This book owes its existence to a large group of people who have not only talked about their working lives but who have also helped in its production in many different ways. It brings together work started by members of an Adult Education Class arranged by the University of Keele, several reports of discussions independently arranged by Rowena Lovatt on behalf of the Leek and Moorlands Historical Trust, together with material collected by members of the Leek and District Historical Society. Tape recordings made for the late John Levitt by members of one of his study groups on dialect have been made available by his widow. Numerous photographs and documents of various kinds have been supplied by people interviewed or taken from the large archive held by the Leek and District Historical Society to which many generous gifts have been made. Where possible, those providing the illustrations found in this book are acknowledged below with thanks, but the Leek and District Historical Society offers apologies for any failures in this respect.

In addition to those already named, Norman Webb and the late Carolyn Busfield have made a large contribution to the preparation of the edited interviews by undertaking the task of transcribing tape recordings. Joy Craddick is also thanked for proof reading work and the Border History for the bursary awarded in 2005

Leek and Moorlands Historical Trust has generously provided the necessary financial backing to enable this book to be published. Its activities over many years have been devoted to the cause of creating a Heritage Centre for Leek and supporting publications of this kind is another way of bringing to public attention the wealth of material which should be permanently available for display to residents and visitors town alike.

The Society and the Trust are grateful for permission from the editor of the Leek Post and Times to reproduce photographs on pages 34 and 59; from Digby Martin for John Martin (Staffs) Ltd photographs on the covers and on page 76; from the Staffordshire and Stoke-on-Trent Archive Service for the illustration on pages 51, 66 and 74. Other photographs are the work of or have been supplied by Paul Anderton (Contents page and pages 10, 11, 12, 25, 26, 37, 57, 60, 66, 70), Victor Barlow (pages 38, 42) and George Keates (page 26). Thanks are also expressed for additional illustrative material to Rowena Lovatt for her drawings and to John Newall, Ramon Lovatt, Eileen Andrews, Eddie Barnett, Norman Williams, Norah Clarke and various donors of books and photographs held in the Leek and District Historical Society's archive.

Editorial supervision, design of the book and responsibility for all errors was in the hands of Paul Anderton who acknowledges the valuable support of the chairman of the Leek and District Historical Society, Robert Craddick, and the chairman of the Leek and Moorlands Historical Trust, John Newall.

Front cover photographs : Job White & Sons Finishing Room in the 1930s photographer not known ; an unknown girl machining in 1964 from a collection of John Martin (Staffs) Ltd photographs donated to the Leek and District Historical Society.
Back cover : fettling a circular knitting machine 1964 in John Martin(Staffs) Ltd collection.

CONTENTS

Chronicles
The Journal of the Leek and
District Historical Society

Introduction

The people who speak to you in this book have only one thing in common. They all worked in Leek in one part or other of the town's textile trades. Accident rather than anything else gives them a unique place in the history of local industry for they have not been selected in any particular way. They are here, however, to go some way towards filling a gap in the historical record. We are all familiar with buildings as evidence of the past, and we can easily find photographs of mill interiors with workers standing by their machines in a suspiciously posed fashion suggesting they were on their best behaviour. What is missing is the spoken account of what a working life involved. This book will serve its purpose if it encourages more people to record their memories of what they did to earn their wages, and how they experienced the daily round of chores spiced with moments of humour, drama, conflict and pleasure.

Histories of Leek's textile trades have been told in many ways, and from several different standpoints. They all depend on collections of evidence. There's only one substantial history of a particular firm - W.Tatton & Co. - and only one man has been the subject of a full-scale biography. Sir Thomas Wardle won fame far outside the town and dominates the history of the dyeing section of the trade. There is one outstanding absence, however, which unbalances all that has so far been written about Leek's textile trades – the voice of the employees. This series of individual recollections from people whose working lives started, in some cases, in the 1920s, mostly covers the years after the Second World War. Each person has responded to questions put by an interviewer and in most cases the discussion has been recorded on tape and transcribed. Left in this form, no matter how valuable as historical evidence, the conversations don't make for easy reading. The tapes and transcripts are preserved in the archive of the Leek and District Historical Society, but to give some impression of what working lives could be like the interviews are here presented in an edited version. Where possible each individual has seen the result of editing and removed errors.

Some of the recordings were made more than a decade ago and not prepared for publication until long after contact has been lost with the person concerned. It was always understood that the interviews were for purposes of publication but sincere apologies are due to any individual who has not had the chance to give permission for the final version as published here. Every effort has been made to re-establish contact because it is considered most important that future generations should know the names of the interviewees. Those entered in this book go down in history as representatives of the thousands of men and women, over the centuries, who have done the work that made Leek a town with an international reputation for its silk threads, stockings, braids, woven tapes, knitted fabrics and ladies' underwear – and that's just for starters.

Eileen Andrews

interviewed October 1987

Mrs Eileen Andrews started work at the age of fourteen in 1934 at Ben Hill's in Burton Street - more formally known as William Hill & Co., Star Mill. She had been born in Leek and her family name was Bould. Eileen had just left the Council School, the one built in 1914 in East Street by the County Council where the older classes had been formed into a senior school in 1931. She lived in London Street, in a 'two up and two down', on the opposite side of the street from the cottages with workshops over. Her father was a butcher. It was her grandfather who found her first job, in Star Mill, as he was an overlooker or a supervisor in what Eileen called the 'hard silk' winding room.

"Well, my grandfather was the overlooker, you know, so he got me the job there. He asked the boss if he could start me on and he started me on there. I never told any of my friends what I did because they all went into mills, you know, doing overlocking and machining. Winding silk was a bit, eh, I don't know, downgraded somehow - because, you know, it was similar then to what it is now. There was not much work about - if you could get a job you took it. And my father was out o' work at the time. So eh, you know, my mother was glad of me to go to work, at anything." Eileen's mother had no wage, and there were two younger children, so Eileen was the breadwinner for a time.

"The silk was in hanks. It was kept wet because if it dried out it went brittle and broke, y'see. So, it was kept in skips, and it was soaking wet, and they covered it up to keep it wet. And then we put the hanks on to what they call a swift with sort of pieces of string that you could pull up and down to tighten the hank up." The winding-frame on which Eileen worked was electrically driven and had 25 swifts from each of which the silk was drawn and wound upwards on to a bobbin. She was taught how to load the swifts and keep the bobbins running continuously by the six older women in the room who had their own frames to attend to as well. They were in their fifties, Eileen now remembers, and she was the only girl.

Eileen's grandfather was the only man in the workroom and he spent a good deal of his time picking silk. "He used to pick the silk. Y'know, the silk has all little tiny bits when it's taken off - it's wound off the silkworm, the sort of cocoon, isn't it - there gets little bits in it. And they had a sort of pair of tweezers and picked all the little bits out, y'know." Eileen chuckled when asked about her grandfather keeping his eye on the women and making sure that they kept hard at work. "And I went on the silk doubling after I'd

Picking silk in the 1930s

learned to do the winding. And I went on the doubling which was harder, really, because you was doubling so many threads, y'know, three or four threads." This was on another very similar machine in the same room, and still supervised by her grandfather. Again there were only a small number of such machines, all operated by women much older than Eileen. The only other sections of the business were one for silk twisting, after which the silk yarn was sold on for dyeing, and a parallel department which wound cotton on to bobbins. This was all conducted in a single-storey building in Burton Street, and when Eileen began there the firm was only working short-time - from 9.00am until 4.00pm "which was very good for me, really, going straight from school." She went home for a mid-day meal made by her mother at 12.30pm to return at 1.30pm.

The business belonged to the Burton family, and it was the son, Harold, who had an office on the premises. "You know, people were really frightened of bosses in those days. You know, and if he came in word quickly went round - 'Mind, he's here', you know. And people never even dared to look at 'im. That's what I now find amazing, you know. They used to say, 'Don't look at him when he comes in'". Fortunately, perhaps, he didn't walk round very often and was, in any case, as Eileen now remembers it, not very strict on timekeeping. Her grandfather grumbled if she was late, but more because it seemed to reflect on him than anything else. There were no penalties for lateness, although they all 'clocked in'. "They was very easy like that on time, y'know. There was no closing you out or anything like that."

Eileen was only caught slacking once by Mr Hill, she thinks, and that was " when I was reading the paper. There was something - there was a picture in the *Leek Post*. All the women there had had a look at this picture and then it was my turn. It was something interesting. I can't remember what it was. So they passed this paper to me and I was just looking at it when he walked in. Of course, I was looking at that and didn't see 'im. And 'er whether - I don't know what he did because I was looking at the paper, but one of the women said, 'Er, Mr. Hill wants yer'. And that was the first thing I knew he was there, y'know. So I went to see what he wanted me for. Thought I was going be promoted or something. And, er, he said to me, 'Haven't you got any work to do?' He said, 'You must get on with your work and not read paper'. I felt awful."

Winding and doubling frames, running continuously in one long room, were extremely noisy. "Oh yes. Terribly noisy. Yes.

Eileen Andrews aged sixteen years

You couldn't really hear one another speak. We got into the habit that you could tell what people said by the mouth. You were sort of lip reading what they were saying - over the top of the machines, you see, because you'd be one side the machine and across the machine."

There were some busy times. One came in December. "Once at Christmas time they had some work to do - but that was in the cotton part of the mill, where they did the cotton. And I wasn't a cotton winder, but they said once you'd done hard silk winding you could do anything. So, they asked me to go on this cotton winder because they'd got this work to get out. And it was Christmas Eve and the girls in the cotton department had had glasses of wine. I know we worked over that night 'till about seven o'clock. And 'er, there was no bosses there. So, while we were working we were drinking the wine. I remember that was the first time I got drunk. I was really ill and felt terrible all Christmas." This is a story Eileen can still chuckle about.

Remembering the older women she worked with, Eileen says, "They was very good to me really because I was young and they was all older. And they were very good to me, really. They used to bring me sweets and things, y'know, and sort of looked after me". She admits, however, that it was dull only having females to talk to, and ones so much older. No other new ones arrived and there were no boys, and though this meant it was cozy, "I used to feel it when I went out with friends and they used to tell me what a good time they'd had at work, y'know. I think they'd been working but, y'know, they'd be chatting to one another, having jokes and talking about boyfriends." Unlike other girls, Eileen couldn't make friends during the working day. She worked because that was what was expected of her, and she had 4s/6d [23p] a week no matter which machine she operated.

When an opportunity for change came, she took it. "I worked for about two years and then there was a factory that was very busy and they was offering to teach you 'machining'. So I left and went on 'machining'. That was in Cruso Street, a mill called White's." A friend told her just to go up to the factory and ask for a job "Which I did and they set me on straightaway. Well, I had to work a week's notice, I think." Her grandfather was a bit put out, but she now had 7s/6d [38p] a week to justify the move. "I think we were making ladies' dresses."

"But I was only there a few months when all the trade dropped off. So, 'er, the people who came last was the first to go. So I was on the dole, then. I couldn't ask mi' grandfather for mi' job back." In White's mill Eileen worked alongside girls not much older than herself, doing 'machining' and 'overlocking', and there was some on 'pressing' and 'cutting out' garments, all different things." Some came from the Potteries, she recalls. "They always called them 'Potherbs'. And there was, y'know - we didn't like them and I don't think they liked us. I think, people in Leek resented them coming and working in the factories - because they'd got a lot of concessions - that they could finish work early to catch the bus back

home; and certain days they didn't come in. I can't remember why but there was certain times they didn't come in to work. And the Leek girls used to be annoyed

Eileen some time after her interview

about it because mill owners seemed to, 'er, what shall I say, they seemed to treat them better somehow - appreciate them better somehow. I don't know why. That was our impression, I mean. We might've been wrong."

Asked how she was told about her job finishing she said, "Well, they just came to us one night and said, 'You'll have to sign on at the Labour Exchange tomorrow because, y'know, we've got no work and we're just keeping on the people that had bin there a long time'. You see, they'd got people that had been there for a year or two. So they kept them on, on sort of 'short-time hours'. And, we that had gone there last had to go on the dole." Until war came in late 1939 Eileen did a variety of jobs. "Well, my father said I'd worked at every mill in Leek because I'd go to a factory and before I'd been there long they'd go on short time. My Dad always said I worked everybody up because everywhere I went it seemed that before I'd been there long they went on short time and it was always the last come as went. So, of course, when you was moving around you was always the 'last comer', y'see."

After war started Eileen returned to Hill's and the hard silk department winding and doubling. More or less the same group of women were there, and her grandfather, but the wages she had as a married woman now were about 18s [90p] a week, she thinks. Silk thread manufacture was considered 'war work' and this exempted women from conscription into munitions factories. Silk was vital in parachute making, especially for the cords used for harnesses.

Eileen Andrews is one of a large group of Leek people whose families had a long involvement in the silk trade. Her grandmother told her a great deal about her own father - Eileen's great-grandfather - and his cottage in Mill Street over which ran a workshop in which he wound silk filaments from hank to bobbin on frames turned by hand. His two daughters provided the power! They worked in turns for very long hours. The only difference between their working experience and that Eileen had in the late 1930s was that her winding machines were driven by electricity.

Interviewed and edited by Paul Anderton, transcript by Trevor Siggers.

Winding silk filaments from hanks held on 'swifts' to bobbins was the first of the many stages in the manufacture of all types of silk threads

Eddie Barnett

recorded June 2005

*J*ust after his fourteenth birthday, in 1946, Eddie Barnett left Leek Council Secondary Modern School on Springfield Road and looked for a job. He remembers that little thought was given to this, "it was generally left until the last few weeks that, you know, your school-leaving time came up. Then, of course, it was a little bit frantic either going down to what was formerly the Labour Exchange, or consulting the local papers, or asking your Dad. And my Dad wanted me to go into engineering that was down on Newcastle Road, the old Moorland Engineering Company ... And I did go down there and the wages, unfortunately, were only 17s / 7¹/₂d per week [about 88p] ... and that's why I gravitated towards the mills." In the textile trade Eddie found his wage would be £1.7s.0d.[£1.35] "I just asked around a bit and eventually got round to the personnel office at Brough, Nicholson & Hall and was interviewed there and 'start the following week' more or less." The Personnel Officer told him what jobs were available. "I didn't want the braid shed... my Dad was in the braid shop - that was a noisy, dirty job - so I selected the jacquard weaving section."

"You were put with a trained weaver for a while, a few weeks, and maybe two apprentices worked together ... I did occasionally work with Roy Randles. But, over all the apprentices, and there must have been a dozen of us, there was one man and he was like ... off his looms. He wasn't weaving at all. He was just training the apprentices." Eddie joined alongside two others, but there were already several apprentices part-way through their training, all supervised by Harold Gleeson. They signed indentures, "but not to the extent of how apprenticeships used to be where some of the money that you earned went to the man who was doing the training. That was well before my time, well before. So I just got the weekly wage, well we all got the weekly wage, and we were just trained by his good nature, as you might say. They made you have one loom, a small loom, at first, - keep your eye on everything, then you gradually graduate to more - until you got to what they call 'a part', y'know - maybe two looms ... or two big looms were 'a part'.

York Mill jacquard weaving room at Brough, Nicholson and Hall in the 1930s

You worked your way up then. Maybe, then, in fact, when you were eighteen or nineteen you'd come on piece-work and you'd earn quite a good wage."

The jacquard looms Eddie worked on were so-called after their French inventor. In his case they were designed to produce up to twelve narrow tapes or ribbons in parallel, but separate from each other. All were the same pattern and were intended to be cut into short lengths at a later stage. "Bookmarks, woven labels, book tabs, you know the old-fashioned book tabs. Anything that required a woven name in with regard to a trademark. And some of them were labels for raincoats like Aquascutum. Burberry's was one customer. There were several big customers that are no longer in vogue now. They've all gone ... blazer badges, black blazer bindings which all the kids - when they went to these private schools - all had, mostly yellow and black, yellow and black round the cuffs. But different schools had different colours. So there was a lot of trade, y'know - 'small-wear', in the small- wear trade like. There were a lot of different things." The firm also wove silk pictures to commemorate particular occasions, but Eddie remembers those as special, and infrequent, items requiring different looms.

"We had one day off - release - to school, to Leek College of Further Education and we

took textile technology there. I think we went for about two years - two and a half years - one day-a-week release. We did get a certificate."

Brough, Nicholson and Hall had many jacquard looms. "There was, maybe, four big rooms. One in London Mill, the top floor of London Mill, the top two floors in York Mill, and the Concrete Mill that stood by the Fountain Inn there. I was in all of them at different times ... and then there even some at

London Mill, part of Brough, Nicholson & Hall

Cheadle where the women worked ... and there was a little bit of resentment because it was always a man's, what shall I say, a man's job - a little guild but, of course, eventually women came in and they were just as nimble as we were. And, in fact, in some cases they were much more nimble. But they did tend to run more looms - more high-speed looms." New looms to meet changed demand went into the newer mill buildings and women were brought in to work them. Cheadle mills were better suited to change than the firm's Leek buildings. At Cheadle, that "was all the - all fashion stuff. And, of course, when another firm took over the company they wanted everything on to one floor, with the high-speed looms. So we were like - some were made redundant and some had to go down - I was lucky enough to go down to Cheadle with several more weavers at that time. And the old things were all broken up because they were too slow, y'see."

When remembering his early years of working, Eddie Barnett thinks of managers as fairly remote people - "aloof " was his word. They didn't go round to talk to the weavers - not to hold conversations at any rate. He remembers Fred Smith. "The manager there was Fred Smith: a big tall, plump chap that wore grey

Original designs for jacquard weaving were transferred to squared paper by colouring each square appropriately. The paper patterns for a silk book-mark on the left and narrow braid below were donated to the Historical Society after the closure of Brough, Nicholson & Hall. The width of the actual braid was 2.5 cms, that of the pattern was 10.4 cms.

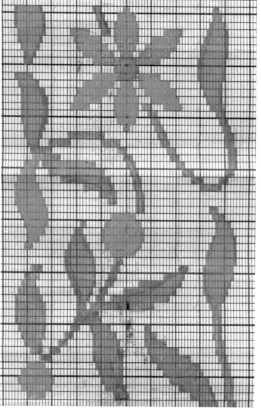

Below
Decorative silkette braids in a
Brough, Nicholson & Hall
sample book about 1910

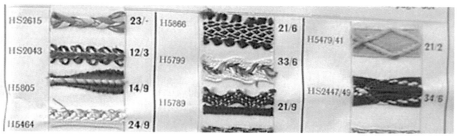

pinstriped trousers and a black jacket and white collar and tie. He just sat on a stool actually and - supervising the girls mostly downstairs ... he didn't have an office as such. He sat at one end of a counter and stared loosely round." His girls were cutting the tapes into lengths and packing boxes for particular customers.

"There was a union - Amalgamated Society of Textile Workers and Kindred Trades (ASTWKT) - Bert Lisle was the president." Eddie's subscription, probably 7d [3p] he thinks, was deducted from his wages. The union did negotiate annual wages. "We did get the hours down. For, I mean, when I started work there I'd be working - as a working week - a full working week would be 48 hours. That was including Saturday morning within the weekly wage. And then I think, 'cos when I left the work the hours were down to 37. We lost ten hours off the working week in my working lifetime." At first, work started for Eddie at quarter to eight in the morning and went on to "six o'clock in the evening with an hour out for dinner ... we had two breaks - one in the morning and one in the afternoon, quarter of an hour each." There was a canteen in the lower part of the mill in Well Street, open at dinner-time, and "a tea trolley came round with a tea urn" at break-time. Weavers could shut down their looms during dinner break, but otherwise had to drink tea, or sit and read the paper, when the looms continued. It was a nice judgement as to how long a loom could be left before a thread broke or a shuttle needed replacing!

Eddie distinctly recalls "a little York Mill Sick Club. Everybody that was in the mill and in the union paid so much per week into it. And then, if you were sick during the year you could draw, I think it was five shillings, I think it was, per week. It was only like in our department ... two shop stewards had it, kept the books straight n'all. Yes, and they all got elected every year." In fact, it seems the club was only for jacquard weavers who saw themselves as Èlite workers - "because it was an Èlitist type of job, y'know ... I think it was, at the time, the best paid job in the textile industry ... the older weavers, as I remember, came to work with - quite well dressed -

Labels for clothes suppliers were woven on jacquard looms

y'know - clean collar every morning and tie - nice waistcoat on and trousers".

As to holidays, apart from the statutory days at Christmas, Good Friday and Easter Monday, Eddie remembers the one week in August when all the mills closed. "And then gradually, there was great delight when it was expanded to a fortnight's holiday, y'know. That was one of the things the union negotiated for and won."

Eddie's final years were marked by major changes in the ownership of the mills he worked in which meant he was transferred for a time to Cheadle. He returned to complete fifty-one years weaving and to see the demise of his trade in Leek.

Interviewed by Cathryn Walton, transcript by Trevor Siggers and edited by Paul Anderton

Minnie Webb

a report of an interview with Rowena Lovatt

Minnie Webb started work as an errand girl at Brough, Nicholson and Hall in 1933, at the age of thirteen, for 8s/6d [43p] a week. Then she became a machinist in the underwear department where the manageress, Mrs. Mellor, was rather a tyrant. She had little patience with anyone and was extremely reluctant to give out new needles when one was broken. This meant loss of earnings if you were sitting there doing nothing until she brought one to you.

Minnie had only been at work for twelve months when her father died and her youngest sibling was born. A few months later, her mother was ill and had to go into hospital, so Minnie, the eldest of six went 'on the dole' in order to stay at home and look after them. She had to go and 'sign on' every day (where the Co-op used to be at the bottom of Ashbourne Road), and she got into trouble with them when she didn't take the jobs that were found for her. Her brother was earning fifteen shillings [75p], she had dole of five shillings (25p) and her mother had twenty-one shillings [£1.05] widow's pension to feed the family. Her mother was in hospital for ten weeks and when she came back they had to pay fifty shillings [£2.50] for the ambulance. Money was so short that Minnie hadn't even enough money for a stamp to write to her mother. They had fallen behind with the rent and received notice to quit, but with Minnie's return to work her mother was able to pay off the arrears and they stayed where they were.

Minnie was very unhappy at Brough, Nicholson & Hall, so she went to work at W.H. White's where she did some 'pulling'. This was pulling the threads out of knitted ribbing to form the welting of jumpers, for example. She also did examining and then overlocking. She always thought of the mill as being very safe because it had a stone staircase and should there be a fire you'd be able to get out easily. She remembered paying 'toilet penny' each week for cleaning the toilets. They took it in turns, and whoever did it got the money; sometimes girls wanting a bit extra would volunteer to do someone else's turn for them.

Minnie got married in 1940 and left the mill when her first child arrived. She started to do homework and while the pay was not enormous she got an electricity allowance - the electrician came to put a special power-point in her house - and it was better than paying someone to look after the children. She eventually had four. She used to get up at 6.00am and work until the children left for school, then continue when she'd seen them off. Minnie's house was a two up and two down in North Street so the overlocking machine had to be in the living room. The four children slept in one bedroom and she and her husband in the other.

She made pants and gloves for men, and small

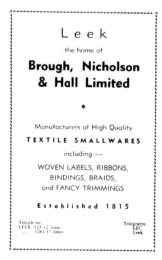

Leek

the home of

Brough, Nicholson & Hall Limited

*

Manufacturers of High Quality

TEXTILE SMALLWARES

including:—

WOVEN LABELS, RIBBONS, BINDINGS, BRAIDS, and FANCY TRIMMINGS

Established 1815

Telephone: LEEK 123 (2 lines) 1261 (3 lines)

Telegrams: LEC Leek

comforter scarves which fitted inside helmets during the war. She had to overlock each end, then, with a rubber stamp, put 'W.H. White' on them and finally tie them in bundles of twenty. Once she had so many in the house that they were piled up to the ceiling! The only time she didn't manage to get the work finished before another lot arrived was when she was pregnant and they brought her 40 dozen jumpers. There were just too many to cope with. At holiday times, she would be brought two week's work at once, because she didn't get any holiday pay and obviously the mill didn't expect her to go on holiday.

The homework created an enormous amount of dust in the house, so when the children were older she went to work for Clowes and Roberts in Nelson Street. After a while, five of them went to work in the Clowes mill in Novi Lane and, as there were so few of them, they had good fun and she enjoyed the job, but her mother was taken ill so she had to finish work in order to look after her.

Minnie felt that her life had been very ordinary with no great 'happenings' in it. Her husband had been in the building trade and was often out of work and she had needed tolerance and patience to deal with that.

A 1920s Arbetter lock-stitch padding machine

Kenneth Bowyer

interviewed May 1989

Kenneth Bowyer started working at William Hill's in 1928 as a lad of fourteen. A next-door neighbour told him about the vacancy. He applied in writing and was interviewed by Mr Ben Hill at Mr Hill's home because he was away sick at the time.

The job was in the warehouse. "You started by sweeping the floors and being a general dogsbody. Then you were taught how to use a typewriter and how to pack parcels. You were taught how to label reels, put the bands round the reels and cops and cones, box them or pack them in papers, whichever it was and generally get everything ready for going out of the warehouse." The main job was in the warehouse, but he worked in other departments to help out.

In his spare time, he was also assistant to Arthur Worthington, the winding and spool room manager, helping him to look out orders from the stock room. "The order came in the post. It was written in the order book, and you went and looked through the order book - so many pounds of whichever colour, or C44. Our big customer Compton Sons & Webb's number was always C. And it was always in stock on the rack. You could take it off the rack and post it or pack it and send it by rail the same day. You looked out the yarn from the stockroom and helped get it through there. You started by knowing nothing, and they showed you how everything was done from sweeping the floor to running the factory. So when you'd been there a few years you virtually knew almost everything about running that mill."

He went to evening classes for two years for maths and one other subject. There was no pre-war provision for formal teaching about the very specialised business of manufacture of sewing threads. He learned by working for one of the firms, "going through the mill, as you might say."

When the war came he was twenty-five and because of his age was automatically in a 'reserved occupation', and that postponed his conscription into the army for twelve months. "The war virtually did away with silk manufacture and we became mainly cotton and spun silk." They had government sub-contracts, their two biggest wartime customers being Compton Sons & Webb of London and Hammond's of Enderley Mills, Newcastle-under-Lyme, supplying the thread for them to manufacture uniforms. They supplied Hammond's with spun silk, as they had done before the war. They also had pre-war dealings with Compton's, large manufacturers of gents' trousers, mainly of grey flannel, supplying virtually all the cottons they used.

In about 1946, the firm successfully applied for his release from the army to take over as winding and spooling room manager on Arthur Worthington's retirement. "I went down to the mill to see Harold Hill to tell him I was demobbed and he asked me to go into the mill straight away. So instead of getting my demob leave, I was at work next day."

When he returned, they were reverting to supplying the general trade as machines for silk manufacturing had been put into storage when half the factory was taken over by the government for wartime purposes. The quota of raw silk they were allowed had to be manufactured into sewing thread at another firm in town. "Some firms were allowed some things, some others, so they helped one another out. After the war, they slowly reverted to their original work."

"When the government moved out, the old silk machinery had to be brought in and set up again. The only new machine they had was an automatic spooling machine, the first one, to my knowledge, in Leek. My first day back at work was spent seeing this machine fitted. While we were bringing the silk back, we had to keep the cotton going. We were so busy with selling sewing cottons to the tailoring trade that they were working 'till eight o'clock every night. We just couldn't produce enough. Eventually, the silk was brought back into play and that was their speciality, silk manufacturing. They were probably the best silk manufacturers in Leek. This was silk thread, mainly for hand sewing and buttonhole silk sewing in top class tailoring establishments. They didn't do embroidery silk."

When he first started working there, they had a small knitting department run by Ernie Hill, Ben's younger son. "It did scarves, jumpers, that sort of thing in a small way, but it closed down on the outbreak of war and never re-opened." By .the time he left, a few years later, the business was run by Ernest Hill and his son, Stanley. Owing to reductions in the bespoke tailoring trade, there was not sufficient business to keep them going, even though they were probably still making a profit. So they sold out to Thomas Whittles, the business at this stage being mainly cotton manufacture. On the sale to Whittles, the business returned to Wellington Mill, where it had originally started before the building of the mill in Burton Street.

"From Hill's, I joined Gwynn & Co in London Street. They had premises on the left-hand side going up the street, opposite Watson's. It was a smaller business than Hill's and I joined as general manager. I was eventually made managing director when the business was bought by Job White. They (White's) had a small braid department, sewing silks. Gwynn & Co. no longer manufactured their own, they bought it 'in gum' from my old firm of Hill's, then did all their own making-up."

When Job White's bought the firm, they wanted pompoms for their millinery. They found a machine to produce them and installed a plant of ten machines with a production of 600 dozen a day, selling not only to White's but to other people all over the country. "As far as I know, we were then the largest manufacturer of pompoms in the world." He finished up as managing director of

Job White's in Compton. They had a fire and had to move to part of Brough, Nicholson & Hall's at Fountain Street to survive. When Job White's went, Gwynn's went, although it was still profitable.

Firms in Leek helped each other, but were also very secretive with one other. They had a Leek Manufacturers and Dyers Association through which they agreed prices, but some firms would undercut others to get one of their orders. When he was at Hill's they had a very big order twice a year from South Africa which had to be put into bronze-coloured boxes. The order came every spring-time, but one year the order did not arrive and this was quite a blow because it was such a big order. "One day I went up to Watson's to see if they could match a pattern that I wanted - a reel of buttonhole silk. And who was unloading bronze-coloured boxes into Watson's but our box-maker! So I knew where the order had gone. And we discovered they'd cut our price by one penny - that's one penny per pound weight - to get that order. We never got it back."

While he was at Hill's he was sent out frequently to get something that matched, or some thread dyed elsewhere. "If you had an item to a small order you wanted dyed to the colour they wanted, you'd go round the other firms in town to see if they could let you have an odd bit of silk as near match to that colour, because it wasn't worth dyeing a small amount. If you couldn't, then you had to get a small amount dyed. Other firms wouldn't let you go into the manufacturing end. They'd keep you waiting at the enquiry place. You weren't allowed to go anywhere near where you could see anything. I've spent hours in Whittles' waiting-room to get a reel of silk off them. They seemed as though they wanted to keep you waiting for the devil of it." Hill's didn't have a dye house until after the war. Then they opened a one-man dye house in the room previously used for hand balling.

Interviewed by Paul Anderton, transcribed by Trevor Siggers and edited by Norman Webb.

Nellie Elwell
interviewed February 1988

The first job that Nellie Elwell had was at Brough, Nicholson and Hall in 1928. Her family name was Clowes. She was fourteen and had just left school at Bucknall where she lived, just below Wetley Moor. Her neighbour told her mother that there were jobs in Leek, although Nellie herself thinks now that she wanted to work in a potbank. The manager who set her on was James Fowler, and on the first day she was rather frightened. Why that was she said, " I don't know. It was the manager I think, he was so strict, you know, and I was terrified. I was running errands for a while, you know, like they do, running errands and then I went into the mill. I got up at 5.45 am and I walked from almost Wetley Moor Common to Townsend to get the bus from Hanley to Leek to arrive at Leek at 7.35am to Brough, Nicholson and Hall, Fountain Street. Five minutes walk to the mill from off the bus and my wages were 7s/11d [39p] a week having paid 6s/6d [33p] bus fare: that only left me with 1s/4d [7p]. I was fourteen years old, and I worked until I was twenty." There were occasions when she would go to work by train from Bucknall station, but she much preferred the bus.

When Nellie was given a job in the mill, and stopped running errands, she went into the hosiery department. This was on the top, or third, floor of Cross Street Mill. "Well that is where they latch hooked. I was darning hosiery - picking ladders up with this thing here", she said, holding out a darning hook. "One of these, you know picking the ladders up and I did that for quite a while. And then I learnt how to fringe on scarves. I did that, and then I worked on a weaving machine." Ladies silk stockings were sometimes damaged during manufacture - described as having a 'ladder' in them. They required repair before they were sold, so Nellie remembers, as "seconds". She and about six others sat around a table, all doing the same thing, with the stocking for mending carefully held by hand, while drawing up from the foot of the stocking any thread which had failed to link up properly with others. She attached the thread in place and repaired any hole at the top. These were made from silk and were "ordinary like, a flesh colour, and they were all the same, no browns or anything like that."

"You couldn't stop us from talking - in a way it was very good. I liked working in Leek." There were other girls of her age, but some were married and there was a mixture of women from Leek and the Potteries. Nellie thinks the Leek girls were "a little bit jealous. They thought we were getting more money than they were - a bit on the selfish side, if you know what I mean. But on the whole I got on alright with them." In fact, Leek women called those who travelled in from the Potteries 'scrawmers'. "They used to say we were scrawming if we did more than they did. It's a regular Potteries saying that, scrawming. It means grabbing." Work started at half past seven and went on until quarter to six in the afternoon. Food for a lunch break had to be taken in. "Sandwiches - they used to make tea in the canteen there, but it was terrible stuff. It tasted like water. Many a time I used to take my sandwiches in the park in Leek and sit alone and have my sandwiches there. Have no drink at all."

"Oh, yes, I must tell you this. Mr Nicholson - he was a great big man. And he used to stand on the entrance when we were coming up the road, and he used to shout, 'Come on you idle buggers. You will be late for your own bloody funerals'. Oh dear, we were all terrified of him, we were really." Nellie can't remember ever being late for work, but she does say that those who were even a minute after time would be told to go away by the doorkeeper. "They had to go back home for that day, you see." She had a works number. "We used to take these checks off a board and give them to the lodge man and then he would put them back when we got in."

James Fowler, the hosiery department manager, is remembered as " a very nice gentleman in a way, but a bit abrupt you know. He was alright. He used to keep his eye on us, you know, to see if we was working alright. And when he was coming in at the door, we used to say 'Hey up, here's Jim coming in'. And then everybody would be working hard, you know." After he left, they all relaxed. He had no works coat to cover his suit and indicate his status, but he was the one the girls pestered for wage increases. They were on piece-rates usually. "When there wasn't much work they put us on time-wages - day wage, you see. When there wasn't any they would send you home at lunchtime - rather than tell you not to come for the day, they would send you back at dinnertime." On Saturdays work ended at twelve o'clock.

There was a fortnight in August when the works closed, but there were no holidays with pay. Christmas Day and Boxing Day were free, but Nellie can't remember any other breaks from work. "I was happy at work. Well, very happy really. I am always happy."

Nellie's career in Leek mills was relatively short. After a spell in the scarf department, teasing out fringes from these knitted garments by hand with a latchet hook, she left altogether, aged twenty, and had short-time jobs including some domestic work. She wanted to train as a hairdresser, but her father stopped that. In 1938 she married a boy she had known from schooldays, and she recounted her early working life with her husband sitting with her when she was seventy-four years old.

Interviewed by Paul Anderton, transcribed by the late Carolyn Busfield and edited by Paul Anderton

Ramon Lovatt

interviewed November 2004

Born in Leek in May 1927, Ramon Lovatt, popularly known as Ray, was the youngest of a family of four. His father, William, worked at Premier dye works in Leek on the stenter machines. Ray's mother did not go out to work whilst Ray was growing up. Fred, his brother, joined the Navy, his sister, Florrie, joined the Air Force, whilst sister Alice married and lived in London. All left home while Ray was still a boy.

Schooldays began at East Street, and then at Beresford Memorial School when it opened in 1935. Shortly after transferring schools, he had an accident, fracturing his arm in five places. This caused some disruption in his school-life and necessitated regular visits to the hospital and Leek clinic in Salisbury Street. Ray completed his schooling in the shadow of the Second World War, at what was known locally as the 'Council School' in Springfield Road, leaving in 1941.

Ray had dreams of being a motor mechanic, but these were quickly dashed when his mother said, "Oh, them new fangled ideas ... go to weaving with your uncles." His uncle Frank was a jacquard weaver at Brough's, and it was decided that Ray should start work there. "When they decided to make me apprentice, the manager, Mr. Fred Smith, who lived off Ashbourne Road, took me to my uncle Frank with a piece of paper." But his uncle refused to have his nephew as his apprentice, so he was taken down the room to Mr. Fred Darcy. "I don't think my uncle Frank wanted to be seen to be doing me any favours. I'd also got a cousin who was apprentice at the time, Derek Graham, in the same factory, and I don't think he'd have anything to do with him either."

Ray's career in weaving had a far from glamorous start, but this was not unusual. All apprentices at Brough's "started at the bottom as a bobbin boy." He remembers this clearly. "They had these skips full of skeins of silk, and you pulled those ... they'd got slats of wood underneath to protect them ... and you pulled

Ray Lovatt is on the right hand side of the back row in a group of his fellow workers crowded into the space between files of jacquard looms

them along the corridors, up steps or up in the lift. And you used to have to take these to the ladies who were silk winders." Ray remembers a complete room of ladies on winding machines. "They undid the skeins and they were wound on individual bobbins. You would leave them with a skip of silk and you would take a skip of bobbins back to the fillers. The filler put the bobbin on an axle and dropped it into a slot ... they were going round ... and then she got the end of it ... took it up through several eyes and wrapped it round a quill. ... A quill is what goes in the shuttle of a jacquard loom. She wound the quills for the weavers ... and she would have hundreds of different colours to wind." Being a bobbin boy also involved the role of errand boy. "You were virtually running errands for everyone under the sun round the factory. You would fetch boxes down from the box shop which was half a mile underground in Fountain Street where they made their own packaging." Ray recalls the underground passages, and remembers them as being lit, with concrete floors and walls tiled with shiny brick tiles in different colours. He does admit there were dark places, like the underground stores, and you could easily get lost at first. "You just had to get to know them. While you were a bobbin boy you were also a 'slay lad'." He describes a slay as "a comb-like structure with a bar at each end."

Ray did not find the transfer from school to work difficult. "I found it such a happy place to be ... it was like a big family ... everybody was really lovely to me." Many people associate early working days with a few tricks to initiate the innocent apprentice. "One or two tried occasionally but I was a bit too fast. I think the only thing that ever happened that I did fall for ... we had tun-dishes which you poured oil in and they used to stick it in your belt. They'd say, 'We'll put this sixpence on your nose. If you can drop it into the tun-dish it's yours.' They just put it there and held it and somebody was pouring water in the tun-dish ... which was rather cool!"

Ray was fascinated by the clothes worn by some of the older men at Brough's, men

probably called back to work during the war. "But what I found peculiar was the dress ... one man who had been retired, Bill Weston, and they called him back because of a shortage of weavers ... and he must have been in his eighties ... and he came in black striped trousers, a stiff front, and a dickie-bow, black jacket, a bowler hat ... and it just seemed everybody was well dressed ... the jacquard weavers were more highly paid than most factory workers ... they could afford better clothes." Even apprentices were expected to "dress tidy ... you weren't actually made to wear a tie, but you did."

The man in charge of braid machines was called a fettler, whereas the man in charge of jacquard and shaft looms was called a tackler. The tackler came to work in a bowler hat, and "you daren't look at him hardly ... he was god

A jacquard weaver's slay as remembered by Ray

The space between the teeth of the comb varied from 20s to 80s to the inch, depending on the width of medal ribbon to be woven. The slay-lad had a knife and the weaver would put so many ends of silk on the knife, and the slay-lad pulled it through, "then went into the next one, held them all in our fingers until they were all in, and then you'd give them back to the weaver, and he'd fix them ... and tie a knot on." All these mundane jobs helped prepare the apprentice weaver, "you was starting to learn how things were done."

because there was only him who knew how to put things right."

Although Ray left school when he was fourteen, his apprenticeship didn't officially start until he was almost sixteen, and was for a period of six years. Ray still has the indenture agreement, signed 23 March 1943 by Ramon and his father. The successful completion of his apprenticeship is signed on another document in 1951,

nine years later. Ray explains: "I had to join the army at eighteen ... I was conscripted into the army and went off to Ireland."

Ray trained under Fred Darcy. "Fred Darcy lived in Alsop Street. He was a really nice gentleman ... he'd got a brother working there as well, Harold. I was with Fred until I went in the army." Ray recalls there were about eight or ten going through their jacquard apprenticeships at the same time. Brough's needed quite a lot of jacquard weavers as Ray recalls about 400 jacquard looms at the factory, with one weaver being responsible for between three and six looms depending on their size. "Some jacquard looms were 24 spaces, that meant they were doing 24 pieces of material all at the same time ... they went from 24, 18, 12, 8, 6, and 4." The jacquard weaver also operated a loom that made Masonic ribbon up

to twelve inches wide, most being in two colours, orange and purple, two shades of blue, or blue and red.

When asked about sources of energy in the factory, Ray explains: "Originally it was a steam engine. That's why they'd got reservoirs i n Fountain Street, to run the steam engines. And when you think it was operating machines half a mile away, four storeys high! They employed a man just to go round oiling!" He carried an oil-can and he'd go on to the pulleys and huge belts. Ray also recalls that the mill was lit by gas when he first started work. "You used to light your own lamp when you went to your loom."

The jacquard loom is a complicated machine and Ray is able to explain this in great detail. They were used to make intricate designs, and produced items such as book-marks and pictures as well as labels. A lot of work went into the design and Brough's employed their own designers. Names of designers that readily came to mind were Giles Smith, father and son Arthur and Carl Vigrass, Bill Cook, and Cecil Bode. "The customer sends a sketch, be it a bird or a mountain range, then our designers project that sketch on to graph paper. It then goes to the card cutter, who puts the graph over a board and he has an indicator. He goes across one line at a time on the graph paper; where there's a colour he punches a hole; then he goes across and punches another hole or several holes; then he moves it up one until he gets right through the graph. In a set of cards you could get anything from 100 to 5000 cards depending on the length of the article you want to weave ... and no two cards are the same." Ray recalls two excellent card cutters, Ted Henley and Albert Chatterway. Ray remembers that Albert Chatterway was also an organist in one of the churches, and describes him as "a little old man but he was a character ... always carried a tin of cocoa ... but there wasn't cocoa in it ... it was full of snuff ... and, of course, in them days nearly everyone took snuff ... they said it was good for your eyes for some reason!" If the weaver noticed a mistake in the pattern as the work progressed, Albert Chatterway "could pick up a label, look at it, climb up to the top ... 5000 cards ... and he'd pull them over and he could actually visualise ... he knew which hole to block up or where to cut more holes in."

Ray has fond memories of the woven picture, 'The Cavalier' "because that was the first thing I did ... I was the first person at Brough's to make one ... I went to Fred Darcy and he gave me a loom to look after ... when I was an apprentice." The Cavalier was an unusual design. "The battens only accommodate six colours and if you check on the Cavalier there are seven," so adjustments had to be made. Ray recalls making a mistake. "I didn't change the shuttle at the right time and I was sent for ... down the office ... Mr. Smith, the manager ... he'd got these six Cavaliers in front of him and he says, 'Look at these, 9d [4p] each them ... they're coming out of your wages ... it never happened again!"

"We used to work six days a week ... so every now and again the apprentices decided we'd had enough work : 'Let's go and play football'! So we'd turn up late ... they used to have a lodge man up Ashbourne Road and he was dead keen ... quarter to eight, door locked ... so we'd wait until he'd locked the door and then go knock at the door, and he used t'open the door and say, 'Sorry, you've had it, you'll have to go home!' Then we'd go and play football ... but then Fred Smith got wise to it ... we did it once too often ... production was down ... so we couldn't be locked out. He said, ' You can't lock them out again!' Ray recalls that during the war Brough's did not close. "I think you were allowed to have so many days off. Perhaps seven days, but it never shut."

When Ray returned to Brough's after his demob from the army, he still had to complete his apprenticeship and so he did another three years with Harry Beech. Ray recalls there

being a shortage of weavers after the war "because one or two had been killed, and I was asked to go on some shaft machines up in London Mill, making ribbon and trouser braid, that sort of thing ... which I didn't much care for because it was too simple, and it was a bit boring."

Mr. Smith had retired and the new manager, Mr. Bradley, asked Ray if he would like to learn the job of a tackler. Ray was pleased to accept this offer. There was no indenture agreement to sign, just five years practical training. "So he took me to Jack Cooper, who was the tackler then, quite a clever fella'. But I didn't get a lot of training ... I followed him round, but he didn't do any explaining. When little things went wrong people would come and fetch me and I could do those ... anything major they seemed to fetch Jack. Gradually, I suppose, I taught myself by meeting the same problems every day of the week." Ray's opportunity to take on a more difficult job came when his uncle Frank's jacquard loom broke down. "Jack had been on this machine that had broken down, and he'd been on it three days ... and he came back to me ... we used to have a little office ... and he said, 'Ray, go and have a look at your uncle Frank's machine, I'm fed up with it ... I canna beat it.' And I went down and had a look ... I climbed up the ladder to the jacquard ... and there was this cylinder and it was just battered ... a cylinder is full of holes ... 600 holes in each side where the needles pass through ... but some of them were broken, and he'd put wires across, bits of wire ... and I thought I'm not starting on this. ... I knew we'd got some new ones that had been there for donkey's years ... so I went and got one ... and put it on the machine, set it up, balanced it, went down and started the machine up, and my uncle Frank came to me and he says, 'How did you manage that?' I said, 'No problem,' and after that my uncle Frank and all the others fetched me for anything." Ray continued to work as a tackler, rather than operating the loom, and this ensured his detailed knowledge of the jacquard loom.

Weaving seemed to be a man's domain, and

Ray confirms this. "There were no women designers; the card cutters were all men; tacklers were men, but the best paid person in the factory was the warper, and she was a lady." Ray remembers all the warpers were women, and describes them as "the king-pins." The warper had a rack of bobbins, "and she drew them through an eye, tied them on a warping frame and she would turn a handle that would send the warp up a big frame ... and it would go up with 50 ends on ... and then it would come down again ... she did that until she'd got the right number of ends, and then she would use her fingers to put a 'cross' in, so every end came out one at a time ... it was a skilful job ... and if that was wrong, everything was wrong ... they were 'top ladies' not 'top dogs'!"

Ray soon got involved in sporting activities at Brough's. Perhaps the bosses thought they would have happier and better workers if they supported such things. Brough's owned a sports field, Beggars Lane, which accommodated a cricket field, two tennis courts and a pavilion. Ray picks up the story. "We used to have an inter-departmental knock-out which the weavers always won because we'd got most young lads. Before the war they'd got good football teams ... when I came out of the army in 1948 they wanted to go into the Moorlands League. I was the representative of the Sports League in York Mill, so I went to a meeting and they said, 'You can have a team but you'll have to run it.'" Arthur Whiston was the Work's Secretary, and also in charge of all leisure activities, and had to be approached for financial support for such items as football strips. Part of Ray's duties was arranging for a referee and organising the team and pitch. "Somebody had to do the pitch on a Saturday morning ... several bags of sawdust delivered to Birchall to mark the pitch out ... and me and a couple of the players would do it." They played against the local villages and other works teams like Adams Butter. It was the Moorlands League, and playing away matches could be quite complicated. "We would catch the bus on Ashbourne Road, go to Ipstones, get off the bus, walk across the fields to Foxt, play football, walk back to Ipstones and go back to

Leek. If we went to Warslow then we'd have a coach. You had to use the service buses if there was one."

As to special events associated with Brough's, Ray remembers the lovely Christmas parties and the annual firm's dance at the Town Hall. The dances were very popular and it was difficult to get tickets. "I think they only did about 300 ... it was like gold to get them with 3,000 employees." No food was provided at the dance, but Ray recalls "there was a private bar for the managers and directors downstairs in the Council Chamber." There were also Saturday trips to Blackpool and Southport in the summer, hiring as many as twenty coaches, picking up in Leek and the outlying area.

Ray remembers the works canteen. "During the war you could go and have your dinner, whip back to work ... and you'd be earning more money. But when I came out of the army and I started going out with girls I stopped using it. I went with girlfriends down to the canteen at the bottom of Fountain Street, the British Restaurant, or the one round the corner!"

Trade Union membership was "almost compulsory", Ray recalls, but "we never got much out of it." The best rise in wages Ray had was instigated by a Conservative government, under Ted Heath. "He gave every worker a £6.00 a week rise, which doubled our wages in those days ... it was all the difference in the world."

Although Ray returned to work at Brough's, in later years, he did leave the firm for a time. "I actually applied for a job at CWS [Co-operative Wholesale Society] mills on Nelson Street. The tackler there retired and I wanted to be not second top dog, I wanted to be top dog!" He got the job and liked it, but didn't think the pay was good enough for what he was expected to do. "I was expected to do the wages and part of the office work as well." When Ray asked for a rise he was told that his particular department was £7,000 in debt, and was told, 'You can get rid of that debt and the sky's the limit for you!' "So I worked really hard for eighteen months. Don Rushton was the rep and I'd got a section that was doing elastics ... and I started to develop that because I thought there'd be more money in it." Samples were made and Don Rushton returned with orders. As a result, a £37,000 loss was turned into a £3,000 profit, but the rise was still not forthcoming. It was the late 1950s and time to move on. "I saw an advert in the paper for a technician with Bonus ... they'd got a base in Nottingham and another one in Sunderland." Ray's application was successful, and the pay was £28.00 per week, more than double his weekly wage in Leek. At Sunderland, Bonus made modern textile machinery and Ray's job was to go to any firm that purchased a machine, set it up and explain how it worked. This involved a lot of travelling, including an eight-week trip to Leipzig. Ray shares one particular story from this period of his working life. He went to a factory in the East End of London. The Hungarian woman who ran the factory asked whether the machines would make corset elastic. Ray was sure that they would because he had developed elastic at the Co-op mill in Leek. Ray returned to Nottingham to make the warps for the elastic and returned to London. Elastic was made and the lady was "absolutely overwhelmed" with the successful conclusion, but it led to a misunderstanding between Ray and the director of the company. So Ray left, returned to work in Leek, and got his old job back at the Co-op mill in Nelson Street. Ray continues, "I did get a rise ... and then it went down-bank." Apparently, there were three different sections in the factory, braid, knitting and weaving. "They pushed everything into the knitting, so we were the poor relation." Bert Lisle, secretary of the local textile union, approached Ray and told him Berisfords of Congleton were looking for a tackler, so Ray had an interview with the boss there, Stephen Sebire. He got the job, with a wage double what he was getting at the Co-op, plus a travel allowance. Ray worked at Berisfords for about ten years.

Mr Bentley, managing director at Brough's, approached Ray and asked him to consider returning to the old firm. This coincided with a period when Ray wasn't particularly happy working at Congleton, and Broughs were "desperate for a tackler." Ray didn't return to work in the Leek factory, but went to Cecily Mills in Cheadle. "It was all part of Brough's, the directors were in Leek, the braids was here still, and the Sander and Graff ... all the jacquard had been thrown out of the window ... sent to India. Jacquard weaving continued at Cheadle, making mainly labels." Ray recalls this happening about 1970.

He later returned to Leek as assistant manager of the braid made on Sander and Graff machines. "I stopped there till it closed ... ironically it was sold off to Berisfords!" Mr. Sebire did offer many workers an alternative job at British Trimmings, on Ball Haye Green, another factory they owned in Leek. But Ray was offered a job in warehousing, and decided to take redundancy as he didn't want to be out of weaving. He was fifty seven years old. Ray explains the events and his feelings when the final closure of Brough's was announced. "I had been back at Cheadle seventeen years with them ... it was like the end of the earth ... I remember Stanley Bentley came over ... we'd been told there was a big meeting ... and the first person to be taken into the office was me. And he told me they'd got to shut ... they'd got no choice ... so they were making everybody redundant ... which they did ... and I came out of the office and all the women and blokes said, 'What's going on?' I said 'I've been made redundant,' and they said, 'Well if you've gone, machines have gone, we've all gone.' So they'd been warned before they went in what was going to happen."

As Ray continues to describe some of the departments at Brough's you get some idea of the extent of the products and the size of the whole concern, properly known as Brough, Nicholson and Hall Ltd. "I think the only thing that Brough's didn't make in a dress sense was shoes ... there was 'Femina' ... that was Fountain Mill ... it's where the start of the Police Station is now ... they made some wonderful ladies' suits, blouses, hats, stockings, socks, ties ... a lot of stuff was made ... there was a knitting department ... they made coats as well ... everything except shoes", but quickly adds laughingly, "they made the shoes laces! York Mill was all pentograph, which is embroidery, doing army badges. On the second floor were offices on one side, partitioned off. The making-up girls sat singing away, and down here [Ray indicates the other side] was all the filling ... rows of fillers, about eight or ten girls filling, and then Daisy Wragg would be there - eighty five - she was a warper, and Mrs Cooke she was another warper. And then we would have the card cutters, three of them in a row ... and at the bottom end there were shaft looms, ribbon looms. The jacquard were on the next floor, all jacquard except for a tiny office for the tackler. The top floor were all jacquards. Across into London Mill, the first floor was winding and spinning, the second floor was binding, bias binding. I'd got an aunty working there, Aunty Clara. She used to make bindings on cards ... winding it on a card ready for the customer. Above that was winding again, Mrs Corden and Co. And then the top floor was jacquard and shaft weaving, half and half. They were a funny crew up there. They'd got Sammy Lowe." There they had "the most modern machine we'd got ... a

real French jacquard, French made, but they were brilliant. And then we'd got all the shaft looms that were making all the stuff for Northern Ireland, all the regalia for the different clans. We had a hat-band section as well. Eight looms that did nothing else but make hatbands and badges for South Africa. They even took that to Cheadle. Maurice Vigrass was in charge of those. He used to set them up. You had to do so much ribbon, and then you had to go up and put the badge on. You'd have to watch it and stop it, go up, take it off, put plain cards in again. It had to be an exact length, so there had to be a man there to do that. Maurice did nothing else but hatbands and diagonal ribbons. A lot of the diagonal ribbons had got badges on."

Ray remembers Faulkner Nicholson of the original founding family of the company. "He always went to Albert Chatterway and asked him get the snuff box out. They used to have a laugh and a joke together." Albert was one of the card cutters Ray mentioned.

When asked to reflect on mill life, Ray thoughtfully comments: "It just felt as if you were creating something."

Interview, transcription and editing by Joan Bennett

More on the jacquard loom, from the description by Ray Lovatt during the interview in November 2004.

"The jacquard loom stands on a platform. There are different sizes of machine, dependent on how many needles it operates, anything from 100 ends to 900 ends, each end requiring a separate horizontal needle. A vertical hook is attached to each needle, and is in turn attached to the jute 'harness' which hangs down the machine. The horizontal needles go through a block of wood and protrude roughly half inch, facing a four-sided 'cylinder'. The 'cylinder' is full of holes e.g. 600, 900 ... dependent on the number of ends required for the production of a particular label etc. The 'cylinder' rotates and allows one pattern card at a time to 'face' the holes. Holes in the card correspond to the design and the only needles that are picked up are the ones facing a hole in the pattern card. So perhaps only 50 or so ends are let into the 'cylinder' at any one time. Each needle let into the 'cylinder' engages a steel hook and it is lifted up. The jute 'harness' is tied to all the hooks, one thread to each hook multiplied by the number of pieces of cloth you are making on the loom. Each thread of the 'harness' goes through a 'comber board' to keep it in position for the shuttle. Each thread is then is attached to an metal 'eye' and a metal rod called a 'lingo'. These 'lingoes' are attached to the hooks, and they act as weights, one being attached to each thread of the 'harness', ensuring that the thread hangs about a foot off the floor of the platform. All the 50 or so warp ends would be lifted up; the shuttle goes through and the pattern is made. 'Slays' are situated at the front and at the back of a long batten, one slay for each length of labels being woven. The batten goes backwards and forwards and the slays push the weft threads up to produce a tight weave. Wheels and shafts lift and lower the front of the batten depending on what colour thread is needed. All this is controlled by the 'lift box' which is connected to the 'pattern cards'. That selects which shuttle goes next." Ray recalls that when a loom was being set up, lengths of jute cord and metal 'lingo' rods with an eye for the thread were sent out as 'homework'. The home workers connected these pieces together.

Part of the pattern of holes in the cards controlling the weaving of the silk picture 'The Laughing Cavalier' with the original design and sample spools

Joan Johnson
a report of an interview with Rowena Lovatt

Joan Johnson, whose maiden name was Hambleton, was so small that when she went to W. H. White at Old Bank Mill to ask for a job, dressed in her gym slip, ankle socks and bar strap shoes, the receptionist couldn't see her beneath the enquiry window and had to come round to talk to her. She started work in September 1938 at the age of fourteen. Her wage was 7s/6d [38p] per week. She gave 6s/6d [33p] to her Mother and thought she was lucky to have one shilling [5p] to spend on herself, even if she did have to save out of that!

To begin with, she worked in the warehouse. At that time White's made jumpers, cardigans, etc., knitting their own fabric in a large room at the back of the factory where the young girls were not allowed to go, (too dangerous?). Joan's job was to pack the goods ready for despatch. One day, Mr. Sam Garner, a director, put her at a table on her own. It was covered in piles of jumpers. He told her to choose the jumpers she liked best, put six in a box and do twelve boxes. When she had almost finished, he asked how many girls her age worked in the warehouse. She said "Five", and he told her to give a jumper to each of them. Such a nice gentleman made a lasting impression on Joan. At Christmas it was customary to give the time-wage employees a box of chocolates, but when the older women told the younger ones that they would have to give Mr. Garner a kiss for it Joan thought she'd rather not have the chocolates! But of course the women were only teasing. She had two more boxes of chocolates and then the war started and luxuries disappeared.

Next Joan went into the cutting room, because her aunt was the manageress, but she was terrified of the cutting machines and asked to be transferred to the making-up department. Here she fitted in very quickly and soon became proficient on lockstitch, overlock and flatlock machines. But the work was changing;

they were making vests, underpants, pullovers, caps, (with becks on, like the Yanks) all in jungle green for soldiers. Later, around 1944, the girls would work four at a time for a fortnight on repairing underwear from dead soldiers. The holes had obviously been made by gunshots; the garments had been fumigated so the chemical smell was pretty awful and it made the girls sad to think of how many young men had died in such awful circumstances. It also showed the very bad situation the country was in.

During the war the factory worked 7.45am to 7.45pm and the girls would go to the British Restaurant at the bottom of Regent Street for a good midday lunch of meat and veg for ls/6d [8p]. When they came out of work at night, it would be pitch dark as the blackout was in force. One night Joan walked out, cutting across what is now the Park, with tall, thin Mary Tatton in front and fat Mary Tatton behind. It was moonlight and thin Mary suddenly screamed, "The Germans are here!" Turning around, she put her elbow into little Joan's eye and they all ended up in a heap by

Joan Johnson aged sixteen years

the mill wall with a soldier wearing a helmet similar to the Germans standing over them with a fixed bayonet. As can be imagined, they were terrified and then pleased to discover that, under cover of darkness, the Yanks had moved in. Joan's eye was an awful mess; in fact it never got completely better and there were many jokes about her 'war wound'.

Joan paid into the Leek Convalescent Fund and if you were recommended for an operation you could get £3.3.0 [£3.15] and then five shillings [25p] a week sick pay, but this didn't last many weeks. She also paid into the Union. As there was no pay for the one week's holiday a year, the girls had a 'club'. They each paid one shilling [5p] per week into the fund and drew lots as to who should 'draw' - that is if there were ten girls then you each drew a number between one and ten and received your money on the appropriate week.

In 1944 she met her husband and they were married that year .The day they got engaged she heard that her future brother-in-law had been killed ,and the edition of the Leek Post which published her wedding also had the death of her schooldays' boyfriend. They were, indeed, very sad times and Joan feels that girls of her generation were cheated of their teenage years. They went straight from school to doing full-time work with long hours and there was no time or chance to enjoy life. Her married life started in the front room at her mother's house because due to the housing shortage there was nowhere else to go. Everything was on coupons or dockets. She had to use clothing coupons to buy the curtains and the ten dockets a married couple got went as follows: table two, two chairs two, tallboy two, and bedsettee four. Everything else had to be begged or borrowed.

Joan stayed at White's until her son was born. She remembers with affection the comradeship of the workforce along with the air of togetherness and determination, which meant that in spite of everything, not getting big wages or having much teenage fun, they were happy days.

In 1952 Joan went back to work at Mason's. The job involved setting up machines ready for the girls to do the orders. Her son was only small so she used to take him to work with her and the girls in the office used to play with him.

She went to work at Job White's, Compton Mill, in 1955 when she was thirty two. She worked in what was known as the 'Bearpit' because it was downstairs. She was on machines sewing bobble hats and bonnets but by 1955 they were no longer fashionable and the job ended. She had found that there was a lot of 'cattiness' over piece-work prices and so she wasn't sorry to leave and go to work in her mother's shop.

W. H. WHITE
& SON LTD.

Specialists in

LADIES'
MEN'S
CHILDREN'S
INFANTS'

Knitted Outerwear
and Scarves

OLD BANK MILL
LEEK
STAFFS.

Telegrams:
"SUMMIT" LEEK

Telephone:
LEEK 223

3

William Owen

an account of my life

I was born on 3l March 1914 at 29 Garden Street, Leek. Our family at Garden Street was mother, father and two sisters. Dorothy was two years older and Bessie two years younger than me. We all went to West Street day school; Dad went out to work and mother was a housewife who stayed at home and looked after us. At the far end of Frith Street there were many allotments and when you walked down Nunn Street you came to a lot of hen pens and hen cotes. Beyond them were more allotments which joined up with the ones from Frith Street. These hens were all white, and some were show hens which belonged to Mr. Sharpe who lived at 3 Garden Street.

On Nunn Street corner the shop then was a grocers and sweet shop. Shentons ran it. We used to save the blue 2lbs sugar bags, and when we had five or six we kids took them to Miss Shenton who would give us a few sweets in exchange. They would then put some washing soda in the bags, which would be used in the homes on wash-day. Wash-day lasted all day and it was always a cold lunch on Mondays.

Boys played on wagons which were wide boards with two axles and four wheels. The front ones you could steer, and they would be ridden down Belle Vue banks. There was little traffic and not much danger. The trick was to see how far you could ride along Macclesfield Road. On one occasion, I saw in the street a covered wagon (Western style) pulled by two oxen. This was advertising ATORA BEEF SUET.

This was the time that new offices for Wardle and Davenports were being built and across the street from No.29 there was a fenced-in area that was used by stonemasons for the carving of the huge stones that were used in the front of the offices. These included large doric columns and when it was finished I used to think how lovely it was.

My father was on the committee of the Oddfellows Friendly Society (Manchester Unity) .One grand day, in the summertime, all the children of the members were invited to go on for an outing on a narrow boat along Leek canal. This boat was horse-drawn, and we started from the wharf which was just beyond where the station used to be. What excitement there was! At last we were all seated and off we went up the straight length and through the narrows on to where the feeder from Rudyard joined the canal. We passed the white house on the left and went on until we saw a small arch. The horse was unhitched and went up a bank and the boat moved into the arch. It was not a bridge, it was a tunnel. Two men lay down on a plank above us, put their feet on the roof and walked us through the tunnel. I know all about it now but it was not very light in the middle and I was a bit scared in case we fell in, or something happened to us that would not be good for us. We came into the daylight and the horse was hitched up again. How big the tunnel pool seemed from the boat and up there on the bank was the fisherman's hut. We went to Wallgrange and to the locks beyond. It was thrilling again to go down the locks, and to join the Cheddleton Canal which we travelled along until we reached Churnet Hall. Then we played games until teatime. We all enjoyed our tea and then it was off back again on the boat. Going back I don't remember the locks or the tunnel pool or the tunnel. I must have gone to sleep after a wonderful day.

Other high days I recall were garden parties at John Hall's home, Ball Haye Hall, in aid of the Mount Pleasant Chapel and West Street Sunday School to both of which we were regular attenders. A Sunday School outing to John Hall's summer residence on the Roaches; walking round on Club Day - these I well remember - also watching Leek Alex Football Club; going fishing with my uncle Fred in the canal and the Churnet, and at Deep Haye and Tittesworth Pool, until I was hooked on fishing myself.

I had many friends who attended West Street

School with me. There was one I will call Joe. As we came out of school quite often there would be a motor lorry outside the Britannia Inn. The lorry would be at the side where the yard was in School Street. This lorry brought full barrels and full bottles of beer and took away the empty barrels and bottles which were in crates, stacked one upon the other. One day, Joe persuaded a group of lads to get on to the lorry to help the driver and others to fetch the empties and put them aboard. In all this confusion, Joe and his brother got a bottle or two out of the crates that were underneath, put them up their jumpers, jumped off and took them home. They lived quite near at the top of Belle Vue. Joe and Bert were known at the pub. They used to take the bottles back at night-time for one penny on the bottle. This trick was not done too often. Why we helped them I'll never know, for we never got anything out of it.

My father worked for W.W.Sales who had a dyehouse across the gullet from Mill Street Chapel and Ragged School. This gullet ran from Mill Street to Belle Vue and I knew it as Pig Street. The butcher, Sidney Bayley from Derby Street, had a slaughter house on the higher ground above the dyehouse . Later this was turned into a warehouse for selling milk. The name of the firm was Clover Dairies. Dad worked in the making-up room, parcelling the dyed products which he delivered to various mills around the town in a motor van. He even went as far as Ashbourne at times. If I was not at school I would sometimes go with him, so I have had a look inside many of the mills in Leek. The dye house must have prospered because a new one was built on Ashbourne Road named Progress Dyeworks. Leek Engineers now use it. It was built by Mr Turner of Grove Street who had a yard by Jubilee Terrace. The ground that the works was built on used to be a marl hole and brick works. Many wells were dug to provide water, and when these wells were being dug the men used a bucket filled with water to dip their spades in so that the clay would slip off with ease. This must have been in 1923 or 1924, for in late 1924 mum and dad bought a house in Ash Terrace, Ashbourne Road, higher up the road than the Flying Horse. There were no houses across the road above the Workhouse,

just fields that the carter John Burnett used to graze his horses on. These had also been a brick-yard. Dorothy, my sister, still went to West Street school for two more years, but Bessie and I went to East Street School and I stayed there for another four years.

There was a lad at East Street School who was the errand boy for Ellerton's in Derby Street. They were drapers and milliners. When he left school I went after his job and they took me on aged twelve. Ellerton's, and Bull's the grocers, were where Lo-Cost is now. Ellerton's was next to the entry that leads to the Co-op, and Bull's was next to Woolworth's. There were three men in the shop. The senior was Henry Ellerton who was a little, handsome man with a grey beard. His son, Harry, and his grandson, Clifford, also worked there with two ladies, a Miss Bagnall and a younger lady who came from Rudyard.

My hours were 5.00pm. to 7.00pm., with Thursdays off, and all day Saturday until 5.00pm. The first job on Monday was to clean the shop windows, one each side of the door. I also cleaned them at other times as required. String was also saved. It was pulled off the parcels that were delivered to the shop. I had to undo all the knots, retie the lengths and make up into balls of string for re-use in the shop. Other jobs were to sort out and put in the right order hard metal labels that had prices on them -1s/11d, 2s/11d, now almost 10p and 15p. Sticks were chopped for the Ellerton homes in Dampier Street and a new house in Westfields. The principal job was to deliver parcels that were goods that had been bought in the shop. These I used to take to the homes of the customers. The speciality of Ellerton's was an extensive collection of ladies hats. There was a large department on the top floor which was given over to the display of plain and exotic hats.

There were many mirrors which always seemed to need cleaning. The hats, when a customer bought one, were always delivered by the errand boy. They were placed in a huge plywood box which was oval in shape. It had a lid that lifted off and a leather strap to fasten the lid down, and another bigger strap to carry it by. The hats were surrounded by copious amounts of tissue paper so that the hats would not be damaged in transit. There was also a cycle cape to wear when it was raining. I well remember going to Haregate Hall. They used to give six-pence [3] which was a very good tip. As you walked up the drive to the right of the house there was an out-house, whitewashed inside, with a black retriever-type dog painted on. From afar it looked very realistic. This building is no longer there, but I did once show it to my daughter. Stick chopping was done in the cellar. At one time the shop must have been a public house for there were sloping walls that went out under the pavement. These formed a chute which barrels could be rolled down into the cellar. Round the walls were stillages which took the form of brick pillars with large slabs of stone on the pillars to form a shelf. This went most of the way round the walls and was cold. Over the entrance to the beer chute were two wooden doors which were flush with the pavement in the street. They were not a very tight fit and as folks walked on them it was very noisy in the cellar. It could be likened to sitting inside a drum. The pay for this job was four shillings [20p] a week. I liked the job very much and at times tips were plentiful. I did it for two years until I left school.

It was in 1928 that I left school and I found employment at the Old Works, Leekbrook. Mr Horace Bowcock was the manager of the hosiery department, and he was a friend of my father. I have mentioned our association with the Mount Methodist Chapel on Clerk's Bank where Mr Bowcock also attended, so I was known to him. When I went for the job I asked to see him and he gave me a job in the hose pressing department, also known as the trimming department. I had to be prepared to work also in the stocking dyehouse if I was needed. It happened that for most of the time I worked in the trimming department. This was where silk stockings were pressed. There were two types - circular, which had rounded toes and heels and were cheaper to buy in the shops than the fully fashioned ones, which were also dyed and pressed. Hosiery was dyed at the Old Works from as far away as Leicester. A van went every day to Leicester to take back the finished products, and returned with another batch to be dyed.

When I started work I was till wearing short trousers. There were no initiation ceremonies or things of that nature. As a new boy you might have been sent to the engineering department to ask the store man for a long stand. The reply to this was, "Right, wait over there." How long this wait would be would be up to you. He might say you have stood long enough, or else wait until you asked him again for the long stand, which was embarrassing when you got back to your work place.

The working hours were 7.45am to 12 noon: one hour dinner; and then 1.00pm to 5.15pm. If you were on the time rate of pay, for three quarters of an hour's work on overtime you were paid for one hour. This we knew as 'time and a quarter'. Overtime came at both ends of the day. In the morning, you could start at 6.15am or 7.00am, and in the evening you could finish at 6.00pm. When you got to work you would peg on with a time-card which you put into a slot in the time-clock (Bundi), press down a lever to print the time in blue ink. If you were late it printed in red ink and if you were in the red you would be stopped a quarter hour on your wages .

When you pegged on, the girls would go one way and the men would go into a place known as the 'Foxhole'. You first went through a kitchen into a cloakroom to hang up your outer clothes, put on your overalls and clogs if you wore them, and to leave your food in your satchel or case until meal time. If you had something to cook, be it bacon and egg, sausage or a pie to warm, then you would put this on your plate and put it in a cupboard and Mrs. Pegg would cook them. If you had an egg to boil you would put your name on it and it would be boiled for you. Water was boiled to make tea. As far as I know nothing in the food line was ever stolen.

As lunch-time came round bells would ring and you would leave your work place and collect your meal if it was a cooked one, or your 'snappin' bag (food bag) from the Foxhole, and go to the canteen. The men's canteen was on the other side of the main road. It was a large shed containing scrubbed wooden table-tops, on trestles, with forms to sit on. It was very basic. On the each side of the canteen was a small railway carriage.

Before lunch on Friday mornings we received our wages. These came in a transparent cellophane envelope. The one pound notes were folded so that you could count them, and there was also a wage slip folded so that the total amount of wage could be read without having to open the packet. A dyer's labourer's wages in 1939 was 47s/6d or £2.38p in today's money.

In the men's canteen on Friday lunch-time it was a special occasion for the gamblers, for Tom was a bookmaker and in one corner of the railway coach he would run a game of Crown and Anchor. This consisted of a board marked out in six sections, and on four of these were painted the four different aces from a pack of cards. In the other two, one contained a crown and the other an anchor. He had three dice and all of them contained on each side the six symbols mentioned earlier. He would throw the dice and he paid out on the money in the corresponding squares at two to one.

Just beyond the old works, on the new works' side stood the Travellers' Rest. This was kept by Mr. and Mrs. Delves, who also moved to the new Travellers' Rest when it was built. On Fridays at lunch-time you could buy home-made meat and potato pies that Mrs. Delves had made but these had to be ordered as there was a limited number. In the area there was also a grocer's and a sweet shop.

There were plenty of buses on the road from Hanley, Longton and Cheadle. Gee's ran buses from Regent Street in Leek. PMT, Proctor, and Berrisford buses were regulars and there were buses with a thick white line down the side - I think they were called White Line buses. All these picked up in Hayward Street in Leek. On Berrisford buses there was a well-known conductor called 'Jack-a-Bill Turner' One day, in Hayward Street, a lady asked, "Jack, is this bus going to Longton?" "Yes." "Well, it says Hanley on the front." Jack-a-Bill replied, "It also says Rinso on the back, but we don't take washing in!" This chap nearly always wore a flower in his button-hole.

All the textiles before they were dyed are known as 'grey work'. When the stockings first came to us, they were hard with gum stiffening and the first place they went to was the grey room. When girls had put them into bags in the amounts and sizes to be dyed, the bags were tied with knots in a special way which coded them for the dyers and those who later worked with them.

From the grey room they went to the 'boil-off' where all the gum was removed. When they left the boil-off department they were ready to receive the dye. There were two types of dyeing machine. One was known as 'the dipper' and worked as the name implies. There was a long rod which lifted and lowered the batch to be dyed in a wooden vat. The long rod worked on a pivot and at the other end it had an eccentric cam that provided the lifting motion driven from a group of shafts and belts. The stockings were looped with string on to thin strips of wood at the welt, and the feet were in a metal grid-like a cage. This cage was lifted up and down in the dye liquor.

The other dyeing machine was made of metal and was like a big drum that stood on its side. Inside this machine was another smaller drum. It had three sections in it with doors which would slide over to open. These contained the small bags with stockings in. The central drum revolved in the dye mixture, driven by a belt from a shaft high above the machine. It would take about four hours to dye a batch as a rule. The stockings were then washed off with soap and water. They were then taken in their bags to the 'whizz hole', which was a building filled with huge spin dryers. In the early days they were driven by steam.

AT
LEEKBROOK
LEEK
Staffs.

Telephone : LEEK 450 (5 lines). Telegrams : "WARDLE" LEEK

Joshua Wardle LTD.

DYERS AND FINISHERS
OF
SILK AND RAYON YARNS AND FABRICS
SILK RAYON AND NYLON HOSE

SCREEN PRINTERS OF DISTINCTION

ESTABLISHED 1830

Finally they went to the pressing room. A press was three flat platforms, one above the other. The bottom one of these 'beds' was about three feet off the floor and had steam going through the middle. The middle bed was fixed, but the top and bottom beds were raised and lowered to touch the middle one. The stockings were pulled on to a flat board the same shape as a newly bought stocking. The board was about one eighth of an inch thick, and the sizes varied from eight and a half to ten and a half, just as the sizes of stocking varied. A 'puller-on' did this, and that was now my job. A 'presser' worked on one side of the press and used the bottom bed Another presser worked on the other side and used the top bed. Each presser had a puller-on, and an extra one worked in between. Eight stockings were pulled on for a 'fill', which was eight boards with stockings on. These were placed on the press and it was raised or lowered to dry them. After this, the presser would pull the stockings off, stack them neatly into dozens, fold them and then start again, for by this time those in the press were ready. This went on all day on piece-work. The finished stockings were then packed into skips and sent off to their makers. My first week's wages, on a time rate, were 11s/ 4d or 57p today.

Wardle's had a good footballing team. They played home matches behind the new Travellers' Rest. Their changing rooms were part of the farm buildings, next to the pub. These were kept clean all the time for their use. If you were a good football player you could get a job at the new works, which was another branch, different from and beyond the old works. There were departmental football knock-out games and, in the summer, we used to play knock-out cricket. There was a sports club. We had sessions in the Leek swimming baths and sometimes, in the new works canteen, indoor games were played - table tennis, basket ball and the like.

There was one grand occasion when a dance was held in one of the large rooms that were upstairs in the new works. Everything had been cleared out, the place decorated with flower arrangements and special lighting brought in. It really was very nice. A good dance-band had been engaged and it was a very successful evening. All enjoyed their night out, with a fleet of buses to take people home. This special dance was never repeated, although dances were held in the canteen sometimes.

When the war came there were several chaps from the old works who were in the Leek Battery. When they were mobilised they marched from Leek to their first camp at Stafford. Their route took them past Wardle's at Leekbrook. Tom Wardle, one of the sons of G.B.Wardle, the owner, was an officer in the Battery, so most of the workers were allowed to go out on to the road and the soldiers were given a rousing cheer as they marched past. Soon afterwards I was called up myself. I never went back to the old works. I had a very happy time whilst working there, and on reflection I am grateful for the privilege I had when Horace Bowcock said that I could work there. Even if Edward Pegg did once say to me, whilst we worked on piece-work in the trimming room, "Bill! If you can't work and talk, don't bloody well talk."

Written by himself

What a difference thirty years makes! These interiors of Wardle & Davenports provide a contrast in working conditions between the 1930s and the 1960s

Lillian Hammond

a report of an interview with Rowena Lovatt in 1997

Lillian's husband worked at Brough, Nicholson and Hall. She worked in the Potteries when they got married but Mr. Jim Fowler, the manager at BNH, said that he would find her a job. For the first month she earned only seven shillings a week because she was learning how to operate the knitting machines. The trouble was that they lived at Baddeley Green, so she had to walk to Stockton Brook station and get the train to Leek which cost nine shillings each a week!. She was twenty years old and the year was 1933. She was very happy there and stayed for the next 35 years.

She knitted rayon at first then, later, nylon. This was used to make lingerie. The pattern in the fabric depended on how the machine was threaded up. Setting up the machine involved lifting ten very heavy bobbins on to the beam, but you got used to that, she said. During the war she made 'sand fly' netting and helped with parachutes if work was short.. Then she knitted balaclava helmets on a circular knitter.

The conditions in the mill were good. The room where Lillian worked had six warpers and seven knitters. They worked from 7.45am to 5.45pm and on Saturday from 7.45am to 12.00 noon. On Saturday they finished work early in order to clean the room and oil the machines and they took it in turns to do the toilets! There were no penalties for being late but if this happened most girls made it up by having a shorter lunch hour, without being asked to do so; it was a point of honour to do so. She did not pay any money to either the Convalescent Fund or to the Union and her wages were brought to her in a brown packet. She did not have a company pension.

The mechanics were very good and fixed up a kettle in their room, hidden behind a cardboard box, and as many of them went to work without breakfast they took bread and jam and did their breakfast when they got there. Jim Fowler knew all about it but turned a blind eye!

There was one boss who fancied one of the knitters, so on April Fools' Day the other girls played a trick on him - they dropped a dustbin lid behind him! It had to be something very loud to be heard above the noise of the machines. They had to lip-read to tell what each other was saying. The boss collapsed; nobody knew till then that he had a bad heart. However, he recovered and despite the disapproval of his senior, Mr. Fouquet, he married the girl.

After a while, Lillian and her husband got a Brough's house in Wood Street which they later bought. This meant that they had only to go a few yards to work and Lillian used to pop out across Cross Street from Fountain Street, nip up the alley by the shilling per night doss-house, over Ashbourne Road to Wood Street at 4.00pm, when she would put her evening meal in the oven so that it was ready when she got home. During the war one of her workmates would say, "Just watch my machines for me. I'm going to wash my hair, I've got a date with a Yank tonight!" To do this was quite difficult because each girl looked after four machines which did 1000 stitches per minute.

At one time, they must have thought about putting the knitters on piece-work and a time-and-motion man came to watch Lillian working. She was very proud that her machines had not broken down while he was there. But he said to her, "It's not to your credit not to have any holes in the fabric", so Lillian said, "Hang on a minute, I'll soon cut some holes for you". But she never did go onto piece-work.

Once, the girls in her room had a meeting and decided that they wanted more pay. They voted Lillian as spokesman, so she went up to Jim Fowler's office. As soon as she got there he said, "I know why you're here and the answer is no". So they didn't get a rise.

On Wednesdays they had what they called "Wednesdays", that is everyone bought four ounces of sweets and they were all mixed together and shared out. For holidays they had one week and as soon as the holiday was over they started paying into the "Didlum". The first week they paid a ha'penny,(0.25p) the second one penny, the third a penny ha'penny (0.75p)and so on going up by a ha'penny per week until the holiday week. One of the girls in each department would be the banker. Lillian used to go to Old Colwyn for her holidays, staying at a boarding house. In later years they used to go for every holiday; Christmas, Easter, Whit and the main holiday. Sometimes they went by train and sometimes they shared the petrol and had a lift.

Life in the mill was great fun and Lillian was sorry when it was time to retire. Despite there not being guards on the machines there weren't many accidents and she only remembered one girl getting her long hair caught in the knitting machine. On the whole, the Company was very fair with its workers and gave them woven silk bookmarks for the Festival of Britain and the Coronation.

Part of the Coronation bookmark design as transferred to squared paper

Norman Williams
interviewed January 2005

Norman was born in Leek 5 July 1914, and had an elder brother. The family moved to Meerbrook but only stayed there for a short while before moving back to Leek. "We lived in Mill St. opposite the Ragged School before I started school ... that would be about 1918. As you looked into the square we lived on the right hand side and then we moved to the double windowed shop which was opposite the Ragged School and Tom Beech's Iron Yard." The shop was a small general stores, "but it didn't pay ... my father went out to work." Norman's father had been invalided out of the First World War because he got gassed. He had several different jobs after the war.

Schooldays were spent at St. John's on Belle Vue and Norman left school when he was fourteen in August 1928. Norman enjoyed school and particularly remembers the garden plots the older boys shared, as well as sporting activities. He had a special affection and respect for the head teacher, Mr Mears. He taught the children aged twelve to fourteen years, "and when school leaving time come, which was only once a year ... he used to go all around the town, all the mills and factories and shops, trying to find jobs for boys that were leaving school ... The year that I left - 1928 - times weren't very brilliant and he managed to get me a job at Davenport Adams, opposite the Dyers Arms ... and he also got Jim Nowland a job ... He lived on the park ... It worried him that he couldn't get jobs for the other lads. Jim Nowland started at Grace's builders yard, in the office."

Norman's first job in the textile trade at Davenport Adams involved much errand work. "I used to go down in a morning, quarter to eight, pick the post-bag up, and come to the general post office, go in at the back and wait for all the letters to be sorted, and then I carried them back and took them to the warehouse at Davenport Adams, and then I filled my time up with all sorts of little jobs, going round the factory." He describes the braid shed - "the noise was terrible ... all the clinking and clanging of the braid machines running round. To talk to anyone you had to shout! I used to go round gathering quills to take to the winders. Winders used to run the skeins onto bobbins, and then it was put on to quills to go into the braid machines. I did that for nine months."

Norman's grandparents worked together at Whittles Mill in Wellington Street. His grandfather was a master baller and his grandmother prepared the work for her husband. It was decided that Norman should be trained as a baller by his grandfather. "After I'd been there a week or two and learnt how to wind the silk skeins on bobbins and do the job she did, she packed it up because she wanted to finish. You had to serve a seven year apprenticeship ... he learnt me the job, no City and Guilds or anything like that, just that you were qualified as a baller." Some years later "my grandfather wouldn't put me on my own because it would have left him with nobody to prepare his work for him or finish it off when he had put the pattern on the top. I went to Tim Whittles and complained about it ... I was courting then and wanted to get married, and pay wasn't very much. And he said, 'Well to

Wellington Mill

be honest, Norman, you're not employed by us. We put your stamps on your card, but actually you're employed by your grandfather. Your grandfather's employed by us, but you're employed by him'."

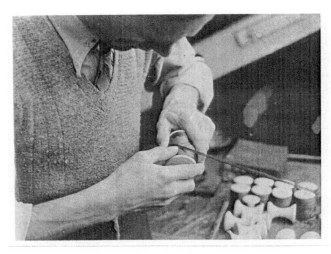

Victor Barlow was another Leek baller who took pleasure in his work

Describing the art of the baller, Norman considers the significance of the pattern on the ball of silk. "I suppose it was a selling gimmick, and it was easy for the tailor to pull the thread off ... six or twelve threads together, and we did have one customer who had nine ... that was a difficult process."

Norman explained how the balls of thread were used by a tailor: "He'd cut the length off that he wanted to put in his needle, put the six round his neck, and pull each one out 'till he'd used them all up, then start again." Norman recalls three master ballers in those early days, two in his room and "another one upstairs on the second floor up."

When Norman started to work at Whittles in 1929 the silk was hand-twisted. "They'd got seven twisters, four on the top floor, three in the room where we were. There was two twisters' wheels at one end, and one at the top where our bench was, and Billy Savage worked that, and these lads used to run up and down barefoot all day ... where they run up and down it was more polished than a dance floor."

They shared their room with the twisters because 'balling' didn't take up a lot of space. Norman, therefore, had an opportunity to see the hand twisting process at close quarters. Twisters "had to have the silk wet ... these lads used to have a spindle with four bobbins on. They used to run down the shade. A skein was 45 yards, so the running would be $22^{1}/_{2}$ there and $22^{1}/_{2}$ back again, half a yard longer than a cricket pitch! They had a frame down at the bottom with perhaps 20 odd hooks on ... and the twister would stand there ... he'd got a big wheel like a penny farthing standing on a frame ... slightly sloping ... with a handle in the middle ... and the little wheel at the top with so many hooks on. He'd take the four ends off these four bobbins and he'd play Hamlet with this lad if he hadn't been down $22^{1}/_{2}$ yards there and back, and put the ends in those hooks before he'd got them fastened on to his hooks ... because it were costing him money! Then he'd turn the big wheel ... that would turn all these little needles round on the smaller wheel ... and put the twist in.

Silk twist came in sizes, 6,8,10,12,14 ... the lowest number denoting the thickest thread, the bigger numbers the finest thread." Norman remembers that the managers would use a magnifying glass to check the twist. "They'd got a little glass in the warehouse and if they had any complaints they'd count how many turns to an inch ... and if it wasn't right it was the twister's fault!" Some twisted thread was made into small skeins, and was known as 'sewings'. Norman recalls, "Most of the sewings were finished off as homework." Many women "used the old fashioned dolly peg ... they used to sit there and put the sewings on the dolly peg handle. They got the sewings which were on skeins and doubled them up twice, and then made a half knot which held it in place. "

Norman worked on the bottom floor overlooking Sneyd Yard. "We'd got two little spooling benches up by the wall, and we'd got a bench at the top 'cos the ballers liked to be up by a window for good light, because there was only gas mantles in them days." A singeing machine was also an important piece of equipment for the balling process. This consisted of a gas jet to singe the silk. Norman explains, "If you've seen silk at all, there's little hairs, very fine fibres ... it singed them off ... it didn't catch fire, not unless it stopped." At this Norman laughs, recalling an amusing incident. "I know the lad that worked with me, but he used to think if he released the jack - the bobbin - it would go a bit faster, but it didn't. It sort of jumped up and down, and he had one or two messes where it stopped and caught fire!"

The amount earned by the baller was dependent on the size of spool and the pattern required by the customer. "There was half-ounce work, one-ounce work, and two ounces ... two ounces was a wooden reel about two inches long. The diamond pattern was the easiest: then there was the double-diamond pattern, which meant that you did twice the length, put the diamond on, then carried on and filled in those spaces. Then there was 'double-rich' and 'single-rich' ... 'single-rich' was known as 'scarf'." Norman recalls that the price at one time for the diamond pattern was 1s/2d [6p] for eight two-ounce spools. Of course, whilst he was working with his grandfather, Norman only had a fraction of that because "the master baller had to pay me. For each pound of work we did at that price I'd get 4d [2p], he'd get 10d [4p] just for putting the pattern on!" The 'scarf' pattern was made by "following on ... instead of making diamonds and leaving a space you followed it all on ... as you turned the spool round you covered it up all over at the same time and not left the diamond spaces. The London agent had a lot of stuff in twelve threads not six ... it was always known as 'double-rich'. With the diamond pattern you just went side to side ... that was one turn of the spool: with the 'double-rich you did it twice. It was a matter of learning to space it out in the first place." Silk thread from the Whittles mill was sent all over the world. "We had an agent in China who sent orders about twice a year, hundreds of dozens. And they didn't buy anything else other than these small little cotton reels. It wouldn't be much bigger

than a shuttle that goes into a domestic sewing machine, but it was wood, and they had ten yards or twelve yards on a reel." Putting a pattern on such small reels was extremely difficult and Norman agreed that you definitely needed nimble fingers. "My fingers have gone all right now, but these two fingers ... with holding it with your thumb and finger ... used to be bent." The little spooling benches and the singer were powered by machinery, but everything else was done by hand.

When he worked with his grandfather, Norman was paid out of his grandfather's pay packet. "He counted it out ... in those days they didn't use wage packets, they used the old envelopes that orders had come in."

Working days were long when he first started. "Forty-eight hours a week ... Monday to Friday quarter to eight to quarter past twelve; half past one to quarter to six, and then to make the 48 you did four and a quarter on a Saturday finishing at twelve o'clock." In the early years there was no clocking in. "It was years after when they had a 'bundi' [colloquial term for clocking-in machine] put in at Whittles. The doors were open in a morning and Albert Hawes was like a timer. At quarter to eight he'd stand out to see if anyone was coming up the yard. There was a big strong gate against the side of the building and you used to come in there. He'd just look if anybody was coming and then just lock the door ... go round with his register ... check everybody in ... and then about five to eight he'd open the door again." Anyone arriving then would lose a quarter of an hour, "they'd be checked in from eight o'clock instead of quarter to eight". But, Norman added, this didn't matter for workers such as coppers, spoolers, doublers and winders because they were on piece-work, and were paid for the amount of work completed, not by the hours worked.

When his grandfather left Whittles, Norman "stepped up on my own straight away", but he didn't have an assistant. "I did my own ... I did the whole process from beginning to end." Once working as the master-baller, Norman was able to earn more money but continued to be paid piece-work. "If you were on one-ounce work you wouldn't do as much as if you were on two-ounce work.

Two-ounce work was the best paid for the baller ... going back to old money before decimalisation, you got 1s/8d [8p] a pound, that was sixteen reels for 1s/8d ... you got 1s/2d [6p] for eight reels of two-ounce." Norman remembers that they were always pleased to receive the orders from one particular agent, W. O'Braid from Australia, "who sent orders two or three times a year, and it was all this good work."

Norman always walked to work. He lived in Mill St when he started work, "so it was easy to go to Davenport Adams, and it wasn't so bad going to Whittles, up that gullet at the side of the Ragged School, and the other gullet. Then we moved into Gladstone Street eventually ... that was good for me." A lunch break of one and a quarter hours meant that many local people went home and this was true for Norman."I come out at quarter past, and went home ... 'cos when I was married I came up here [Carlton Terrace] ... I used to reckon quarter hour walk up, quarter hour walk back, and lunchtime in between."

Given the long hours, Norman agreed that holidays were very special but not very frequent. "We had ten days holiday a year ... you had one week's annual holiday in August ... first week in August ... then you had two days at Christmas, Good Friday, Easter Monday, and Whit Monday ... more or less all mills had the same. If you went to Blackpool you'd see half o'Leek there ... that's why I never went!"

At the start of the Second World War Norman was the only baller at Whittles. "The other fella, Harry Sutton, had been called up. Everybody were ordering ... didn't know how long the war were going to last. ... We were pushed out of the place." Norman explains that he was taken ill in 1940. "I was working 'till quarter to ten every night on balling ... just give me enough time to get in for ten o'clock, have a bit of supper and go bed ... and I was making a bit of money ... 'cos I'd got married then and we were living with Alice's parents.

We were saving quite a bit of money ... saving to buy us own place".

One night, after Norman finished work at the mill, locked up and walked home, he collapsed. "I'd got double pneumonia ... and Dr. Peperdine was sent for. He thought there was something the matter with my chest and my back ... and he took an infusion and sent it away ... and that was TB fluid. So I finished up five and a half months in a sanatorium ... I went to Prestwood, that's close to Stourbridge. Alice come a time or two. She couldn't come very often ... we'd got Brian then. I went into this sanatorium on Easter Monday 1940 and I come home about a week before August." Norman recalls that the weather was "gorgeous" that summer and remembers walking round the grounds at the sanatorium. "It must have been a big estate at some time ... it was a nice place. There was semi-circular pavilions tiered up and I was right at the top. Sister Shute was playing tennis ... and when she come on her rounds next day I said ,'Is there any chance of having a game of tennis?' And she said, 'Ooh, you'll never play tennis again!' ... I had my medical papers [for war service] whilst I was in there and the head doctor filled them up. The head doctor sent for me the day before I come home and he says 'I believe you're a sportsman, young man ... well let me tell you this ... your sporting days are over ... what you've had has affected your lungs and heart'."

On his return to Leek, Norman "had a couple of weeks when I went across the park" and he sat watching men playing bowls. On one of these occasions he met Bert Smith, who worked as a tailor for Percy Trafford. Norman recalls, "P. M. Trafford had a place just below where Kwik Save was, opposite where Leek Post was ... where the entrance was up Pickwood [Road]. Bert was from down south ... Bournemouth way." Bert was a bowler. "There were three of us and he come to us and says, 'Would you like to make us up?' and I said, 'I've never played.' He says, 'I'll show you how.' And luckily he was a left-hander and that started me off bowling." Bowling remained a major interest for Norman and he has won many trophies over the years. He also holds a number of records. He played in the final of

Norman playing bowls in Leek Park in 1948

the Staffordshire British Parks Individual Merit competition on five separate occasions, winning the championship twice, the only Staffordshire player to do so. He also played for the Staffordshire Parks County side in 107 consecutive matches setting yet another record. Norman remembers how difficult it was to survive when the breadwinner was ill. "You got sick pay ... which was nothing ... and I was also in the union, so I got a little bit from there as well. But when I come home Alice says, 'I'm sorry, duck ... but all us savings are gone.' She'd had to use it to live on. And I said to her, 'Don't worry about that. Since I've been in there my priorities have changed ... what I'm going to do now is see that while we're still here we have a good time. And when I'd been home and started work again I went down Broad Street to the offices and thought about going on war work ... I'd already joined the ARP and I was an ARP warden." Norman was advised to stick with his job at Whittles because of his recent illness. During the latter part of the war, work for the ballers "dropped off ... and at one stage I was perhaps only doing a couple of days a week ... I used to go down every day, do the orders and knock off."

Norman continued to work as a baller, but not actually until he retired. "What happened was ... the balling dropped off ... there wasn't the orders." Both Norman and the man who worked with him "filled us time up in the dye-house ... and he went into the making-up."

Interviewing, transcribing and editing by Joan Bennett

A closer look at the baller's art as Norman Williams described it.

After the twisted thread was dyed in skeins, it was prepared for balling on the spooling benches. The dyed thread was wound off the skeins on to large wooden bobbins. The bobbin fitted into a wheel and the whole was screwed onto a jack. An iron frame with two brackets, locally known as a 'risis', was used to adjust the size of the skeins. Norman explains, "You would run each skein onto a bobbin, tie a knot, put another one on this 'risis' ... it just kept running round." Then "you'd got a bobbin full in the singe-er, run it through two rollers." The silk "went from one bobbin to another as you singed it, then you put that bobbin onto another jack, and you spooled it off, onto a spool - whatever the customer wanted. I used to wind it onto bobbins, singe it, spool it off." These spools were placed on a tray and taken to the baller's bench, "and all the baller did was put the pattern on, and then I went up and singed it again. We had a little gas jet and a little wooden handle with a bit of a bar on, and you used to do two at a time, just turn 'em round on this handle ... to singe any hairs that were left on at the top for look's sake. Then we'd got a little roller to even it ... to make it look nice and posh! They called it 'topping up', putting that pattern on. You used to make a knot and stick a pin in ... they didn't tie it ... just a pin - stuck into the knot and onto the reel. We'd take it up into the warehouse where it'd be labelled and boxed."

Victor Barlow took this photograph of the attic 'shade' in which he did balling work. He started by assisting his father at Wardle & Davenports in 1937

Rowena Lovatt

interviewed January 2005

*A*s an eyewitness to some sections of Leek's textile trades, Rowena Lovatt is without equal. In certain respects, her experience reflects that of many women in the number of firms she worked for and the variety of skills she learned. She came to Leek at the age of six in the year after the Second World War ended because her father took a bank manager's post in the town. She was sent away for most of her schooling but after her O Level exams, during a half-term break her father told her he had found her a job with Lux Lux. She was to be trained as a manageress. "Anyway, I went along for this interview and had a look round the mill and to this day I do not know why I decided, yes, I would quite like to go and work there. And so I started January 1957 in the cutting room."

The firm occupied a former silk mill and got its name from the place of origin of the family who established it - 'Luxury from Luxembourg'. "By the time I got there the Goeritz family owned the whole factory. It started off with the top floor when the Goeritz family were interned in this country during the war and gradually took over the whole mill. They must have been an absolute godsend for the Brosters, whose mill it was, because they were really pretty hopeless at running the company. Obviously. That's why it was - going down the Swanee."

The owners of this firm made ladies' nightwear and underwear - "They were Jewish. Very canny. And as early as 1920 they had ... or even before ... they'd seen the way that things were going. And they certainly had a flat in London in 1920. They had an enormous factory in East Germany, or what was East Germany, which was still being shown off in the 1970s as a model factory. Now, whether they got anything back for that, I don't know. But, certainly, they were in this country at the start of the war and they did the same thing with Howard Town Mills in Glossop - started on the top floor and gradually took over the whole factory."

Managerial training started with experience in several different departments. "I went to the Arts School on a Friday, on 'day release', and did my Ordinary Level, City & Guilds, Dressmaking. So that and the O-levels are the only qualifications that I have. I had about six months, I think, in the cutting room and then I went downstairs. I worked on every machine in the factory."

The main production line was for nightwear. "We did mainly nightdresses, negligées, housecoats in cotton and nylon. We did those double-layer nighties, '20 denier' over '40 denier', which had huge skirts, an enormous amount of material in them, at one time. Very, very glamorous actually and a lot of people say to me, nowadays, 'Oh, we can't get anything like we used to'. We did some slips, petticoats and waist slips, and we did knickers and bikinis when I first started but those got less and less over the years and we did more on the nightwear." "Oh, we did all sorts of knickers to begin with. We did these glorious 'Directoire', as they call them, 'Hoover bags' or ' Passion-killers' as they were known, 'cos they came down to your knees. The French

Rowena Lovatt

knickers were known as 'easy feelers' for obvious reasons - but we didn't do knitted ones. The knitted underwear was all done at Glossop."

"When I first started in the cutting room my original wage was £1.10s.0 [£1.50]. After a fortnight I had a birthday so I had a rise to £2.00 a week - thought the boat had come in! I think by the time I went down on to the machine-floor I was probably earning around £2.10s.0d [£2.50p] a week. I was not paid piece-work rates but I was expected to work as fast as the girls who were on piece-work and I could put in ninety-six dozen gussets a day. But, when I discovered that the girl who had been doing it for years could do one hundred and four, I thought, blow'em, I'm not killing meself for eight dozen gussets!"

Rowena's recollection is that the girls on the machines "would probably be earning - £3.0s.0d to £3.10s.0d or something like that. And £4.0s.0d, perhaps, on a really good week, if they'd got a really good job." As to other trainee manageresses, there weren't any. There were lots of trainee machinists though. Learning to use an electric sewing machine to sew together pieces sent from the room where they had been cut out of vast rolls of fabric demanded considerable skill. "You learned to sew on lined paper. Because, when you're

learning to sew it's much more important to know how to stop the machine than start it - because they do something like 6,000 stitches a minute! You had no cotton in the needle. You had to sew four holes between the lines and stop. Four holes and stop. When you were good enough at that you then moved on to shapes which were drawn onto paper. And you had to machine, following the line of the shape exactly. Sometimes it was a sort of - a bit like a clef - a music thing, a sort of curly thing, which is quite difficult to follow. And once you could do that then you moved on to sewing straps, which was a little tiny square of four stitches in a square. You had to learn to do it. You sort of went round three sides and then turned the whole work back to do the fourth side and over your original one again and then move on to the next."

"Something, perhaps, that people don't realize is, you never used your scissors by putting your fingers in the holes of the scissors. You picked them up in the middle and worked the blades between your thumb and two fingers. You didn't have time to put your fingers through the holes and use scissors like most people do - because in my day there wasn't compressed air that cut the ends off. You had to do that individually for each thing. So that again was all part of learning to be quick and neat, really."

WHO HAS A RANGE TO DELIGHT ANY WOMAN?

Lux Lux

New Lux Lux range of nightwear and lingerie designed for all women. For the youthful and the very discerning. The same women you as a retailer are interested in!

Send for the new Spring Catalogue. It's worth looking into!

Illustrated, JOSENA, in sheer printed Nylon. Retailing at about 49/11.

Rowena worked in the cutting room and machine room at Lux Lux. There was a basic division in the manufacture of garments according to the material used. The firm's mill in Glossop concentrated on using knitted fabric "vests and cosy-tops and pants and knickers that are all made of, perhaps, cotton - 'Lycra'- well, they're just a bulkier knit. It's a bit confusing because a lot of the nightwear was 'knitted'. We used knitted, '20 denier' and knitted '40 denier' nylon, millions of yards of it, I suppose, over the years." The difference between woven and knitted fabrics is that between, say - "a polo shirt is knitted and an ordinary shirt is woven. So a nylon nightie would be a knitted fabric. 'Brushed' nylon was knitted - the dreaded brushed nylon. But we used woven as well. I mean we made the cotton nighties as well."

The firm's products were sold under different names and in different ways. Lux Lux was the title used for 'direct to retail' selling. The company's own salesmen toured High Street shops and independent retailers, collecting orders. "We sold to little lingerie shops and people like Rackham's, all sorts. People like Emmy Bailey in Leek bought Lux Lux. So we had our own range - we produced two ranges a year and we had our own reps who went out and sold them. Then, we sold under the Gort label. We sold to Marks & Spencer on the nightwear side. Ritz was used for Marks & Spencer knitted underwear, and when we were selling to Littlewoods or any of the other chain stores we used the name William Broster & Company. This was to differentiate between them all."

"Marks & Spencer would never believe that the quality was the same throughout the factory. It was. We used Marks & Spencer's quality throughout the factory because we wanted a workforce that could be moved around, anywhere. Marks & Spencer never liked this. They were sort of happy when we had just one floor producing Marks &

Spencer's but they weren't really happy until we had Marks & Spencer's being made at Frith Street and everything else being made at Waterloo Mills, 'cos they could then really control the quality. But, in reality, we had the same quality in both factories. We never produced goods which were more shoddy, let's put it that way, for anybody else."

As a family-owned firm, Lux Lux was dependent on a new generation taking over when required. After the death of Thomas Goeritz "around 1972-3 ... his brother Andrew took over and Andrew had a son, David. By this time we had 1,200 employees in the company. We had two factories in Leek, one in Glossop, a very large factory in Runcorn that made 50% of Marks & Spencer blouses, and David knew that there was no way that he could ever run a company of that size. And so, they went to the City. And a man, actually from the factory in Runcorn, borrowed money from the City and bought the company out. So, that's when I was made redundant. A lot of the people were made redundant and they closed the Waterloo Mill in Leek and moved everything to Frith Street. I may forgive but I cannot forget quite what happened because the

A Lux Lux group give their opinion on the latest designs. Mavis Smith second from left

way it was done, it led to the suicide of Ted Wood who was an absolutely super manager. So, I may, as I say, forgive but I can't forget."

The section of the firm in which Rowena eventually settled was the Design Department. "When I joined the company there was Muriel Hall and Mavis Smith in the design room, designing. Not the knitted, obviously, that was designed at Glossop." Garment design for mass-manufacturing methods to meet the criteria of a variety of customers was a demanding business. "To begin with I had Littlewoods' account. At Littlewoods' I had to design four 'ranges' a year. Incidentally, Mr. Wood once calculated that I did one design for every day of my working life."

To produce the sample garment meant buying materials in small quantities. "There were days when I would be buying. I mean, we used to dread embroidery reps coming in - I mean, these embroidery reps used to come in with four or five suitcases, and it was a couple of hours job. You knew it was going to be

absolutely ages. They used to come to us and you got to know a lot about quite a few, particularly the lace people. You got to know them very well. You got to know about their families - and everything else."

"So then, once a range had been chosen we had to make all the patterns in cardboard ready for production; grade them all up; and, as I say, there were these double nighties. Well some of them had huge circular skirts and you had to Sellotape cardboard together and make these huge things. And, also, when on the Lux

Lux range, when that range had been chosen, we had to make patterns and then cut out. I think we did two-and-a-half-dozen of every garment. Well, if there were sixty garments in a range, what are we talking about? - 180? No, 1,800 aren't we, which we would have to make up for the reps to take out to sell."

"You were always twelve months ahead so, here we are now in January 2005, you would be thinking about the Spring, Spring/Summer range for summer 2006. You would be thinking about completing that one for mail order and then that would be followed by Spring/Summer 2006 chain store." Planning so far ahead had special consequences. "I mean, particularly sometimes when you were using like Swiss embroideries and things like that you would buy your Swiss francs ahead and that sort of thing - bought the currency ahead so the price stayed the same."

Designing garments followed a regular schedule. "The first thing that was given to you was the price. This came either from Littlewoods - or whoever your customer was - or from the management if you were designing for Lux Lux. You would probably have two or three different price points. For instance, nightdresses that were going to sell at £7.99, £10.99. or £12.99. So they would probably pay you £5.00 for something that was going to retail at £9.99."

"You had to think of a design, make a pattern for it, cut it out, and then you had to do the costing. Now, costing consisted of doing a small 'lay', like a jigsaw puzzle - getting the maximum number of pieces out of the minimum amount of fabric to work out how much fabric per garment. You had to work out how much lace, how much elastic, how many ribbons, how many bows, everything required. You would list those."

"Then, you had to write down the amount of time it took to do each operation. Things like 0.5 of a minute for a shoulder, 0.75 for a side seam, and 1.25 minutes for a hem. If it was a very simple, cheap garment it would probably take about ten minutes - the amount of time from when the roll of fabric was picked up at one end of the factory until the entire garment was hanging up in its polythene bag at the other - that would be the amount of time of somebody would actually be touching it."

"So, having done your costing, - sometimes you did the costing first if you were doubtful as to whether it would come into price and the cost clerk would tell you 'No, it's come in at five pounds and five p (£5.05p)'. So you had to go back and find a cheaper lace or cut your 'lay' down a little bit. But, cutting the 'lay' was always awkward because if it was for somebody like a chain store they had their minimum measurements and you couldn't go below them. So you'd find a cheaper method of 'make up' - but you had to find something to get that garment into price. Once you'd got it into price then you'd get your machinist to make it up. You'd give her a little sketch and give her the cut-out pieces and she would make the garment up."

"So, you would have to do that for every garment. With Lux Lux you had a little bit more leeway. If it was for something that was really lovely and you thought it looked value for money then the price points weren't so vital."

"Anyway, for a chain store you would do about forty garments, say, and you'd take them up to Liverpool and hang them round the room. And if you'd got a nice buyer, which I did have to begin with - I had a man called Barry Mighall - he would say, 'Oh, yes, I like the colour of that one; Oo-oh, that's lovely lace and ... yes, I like that style - so do it that colour, in that style, that lace, do it long, do it short, do it baby doll, do a pyjama'. Before you knew where you were you'd got whole pages of a catalogue and life was lovely."

"But, of course, he didn't last very long and I got this lady called Mrs. Dyer, who nobody got on with, and she was a bit of a dragon really. So that was when they decided that her personality and mine did not get on well together and I could go onto the Lux Lux range. Actually, they didn't find anybody whose personality got on with her, but that was another point."

"So for Lux Lux I'd probably do about sixty

garments, something like that, and then they would get all the other designers, maybe those who worked on Marks & Spencer's, or whoever happened to be around - we would all go down to the office and have what Mr. Wood called 'The Bun Fight.'. The lady in the canteen would produce soup and sandwiches and things like that. And Mister Andrew would come over from Glossop and one or two of the representatives, and we would all sit round and look at the garments. And it was horrifying because you'd hang something up on the wall and you'd think, 'What ever came over me? Whatever made me do that?' And sometimes, you yourself would throw something out before anybody had chance to say anything about it."

"I do remember once - there was one garment that I'd done - I thought, 'That's foul, it's absolutely revolting. I wonder what came over me.' But, for some unknown reason, Mister Thomas liked it, and I said, 'No, no. You can't have that - can't have it'. And he got up and he went outside the door and sulked, and came in laughing his socks off. So there were lighter moments. We did have fun."

Designing garments for Lux Lux was not done in some remote studio, away from the bustle of the machine room. "The design room was a sort of cage actually, literally, just divided off with chicken wire at one end of the room. It was the fourth floor and half of it was machining and half was the design room. Yes, you would go on the floor quite often if you needed to use a specialized machine. We didn't have them all up there - we didn't have one of everything in the design department like a smocking machine, or the one that did marvellous sort of ruching [pleating the edge of fabric to create a frill]."

"You would have to go down and get the girl on the shop floor to do the sample for you. You would have to go and see the manageress quite often. Sometimes, if it was an operation that was unusual and you really didn't know what price to put in, you could guess very well but you would ask her to make the decision. Other times she sent for you, and you got told off for not putting enough in for making the garment up. You never got told that you'd put too much in, but you did get told off for not allowing enough. So, yes you had quite a lot of contact with the girls."

Rowena particularly remembers one nightdress she was asked to produce. "Mr. Wood came to me one day and said, 'What's the cheapest nightdress you can design?' And so I came up with this nightdress which had very, very cheap lace, and it had it on the hem. It was about two inches wide and it was dirt cheap. Well, you've got to put something on the hem. So, actually, this lace was cheaper than the fabric - and it had the same lace gathered just round this very, very simple neckline. And that nightdress, we produced for 12s/6d [63p]. And it was 'The Kleenex Nightie'. And you sent in two box tops and a guinea, y'know, twenty-one shillings, £1.05 nowadays, to Kleenex and you could have a nightie in one of the colours of the Kleenex paper handkerchiefs. So, we made money on it. Kleenex made money on it. And, actually, it was still a bargain. It was still a nightie for only a guinea. And we must have made 20,000 dozen [240,000] of those and it kept a team going for two years. So", Rowena recalls, " I think that was one of my better achievements, put it that way."

The Kleenex Nightie

There were other design challenges. "But there were times when it was very hard to think of something. Your mind did go blank - but we did used to have these 'ad-clips', they were called. It was a sort of magazine of lingerie advertisements from America which gave you ideas. And you had magazines here. You would sit and look at Vogue or something other. But more often than not you were just playing about with a piece of lace on a dummy and one thing will lead to another. A lot of people say, 'How is it that a lot of designers come up with the same type of thing in a season?' And it's funny: one thing does lead to another, and once you do get on this sort of bandwagon - I suppose it has something to do with the fabric people, their colours and the prints and things, the type of things they come up with, that does sort of lead you, influence you and lead you in a certain direction. So, I suppose that's why - yes."

It was important that Lux Lux designers kept in touch with current trends. One way was for them to take it in turns to go to trade fairs. "We used to do trade fairs. Not so much in this country, actually. We used to be sent - we used to take it in turns 'cos, on average there were three designers and as time went on there were juniors as well. But we would be sent - there used to be one in the autumn in Germany or the spring in Paris. Germany could be either Colgne or Düsseldorf. And we would go to one or the other in a year and get ideas. But, you see, Thomas Goeritz was an incredible man. He didn't believe that you should just go to a trade fair and come back again. He believed that while you were there you should go to the art galleries and you should go to the museums and experience as much of the culture of the place that you were in as possible. He would send us abroad with Henry. Now, Henry Ashford was a fellow Jew and he was wonderful to go abroad with, a really marvellous man. He would make you think about what you were doing and he would say, 'Right, your turn to choose the restaurant. What have you got to do?' And you would have to go down a street and pick a restaurant that looked attractive. Then you had to look at the menu. Had it got the right thing at the right price? Then you had to sniff. And if there was the slightest whiff of cabbage water - no! And then you had to look inside. And if there was a sauce bottle in sight - no! - you didn't go in it. See, it made you think."

"The other thing he said was, 'You are in a strange country. You cannot speak the language. How do you know what is the most important building to go and look at? Easy. If there's anything worth looking at there's always a postcard, isn't there.' But, y'know, it wasn't until years later and I mean years later that the penny dropped as to why they sent us abroad with Henry. We were safe as houses with him. No, we did have some great experiences abroad, there's no doubt about it."

Factory work for the machinists was repetitive and pressured. "One person didn't make the garment all the way through. Somebody would put gussets in, somebody would do side seams, somebody else would put the elastic in or whatever. So it was, it was piece-work - highly repetitive in many ways." Music was relayed over a tannoy system, and conversations could go on endlessly. Anything for a laugh to relieve the strain. "I mean they played tricks on one another - particularly when somebody got married. I mean they did all sorts of things to them. They would get a coat and sew up across the bottom and sew the bottom of the sleeves and stuff it full of waste, absolutely stuff it solid. So this poor girl had got to carry this coat home which was like a great big dummy, sort of thing, a great big body. And they would dress them up in something or - the whole team would go out at lunchtime. Well, when she came back she probably wouldn't be able to get to her machine for all these strips of waste, 'tie ups', that they used for tying up bundles of work, and they would make a sort of cobweb all round the machine so that she'd got to cut her way into her machine when she came back. Oh yes, but it was good-natured fun. They were really a scream in actual fact, quite often. There was one tale of a girl - they all went out at lunchtime and she was really - she had a little too much to drink, so they just put her in the bottom of one of these great big trolleys and covered her up with work and let her sleep it off again - nobody knew she was there like."

This garment-making section of Leek's textile trades was particularly staffed by women. "I would suppose that the majority of the girls were probably between 15 and 25 years old. Although there were, on the other hand, quite a lot of older ladies who were always known as 'Missus'. They were never called by their Christian names. They were always Mrs. So-and-so". Younger women would leave after marriage to have children, and may or may not return. Those who were older, with or without children, were likely to have developed highly valued skills for which they were respected as much as for their age.

"I mean, I'm just thinking of one lady called Doris, who was in charge of the lace department. Now her job was very, very skilled and she was there until she retired.

Cutting lace was a very, very skilled job because you had to cut things in pairs. You had to buy lace in 'left' and 'right'. You'd have say- something with a rose with a stalk. So, on your right-handed lace there was a flower with a stalk sticking out to the right. Then you had to buy the left-handed lace with a stalk sticking out to the left. You then had to be careful to put the two right sides together and you cut your lace so that, on a bra - y'know, the bra on a nightdress or something - then it matched. 'Cos it looks very peculiar if you've got one stalk sticking up all way one side of you, then it sticks down on the other side. It just doesn't look right at all. So it was - a lot of the work was very skilled."

At the time when about 160 girls were employed, there were fifteen or so men - mechanics to keep the machines in good order and men in the stores and warehouse. The factory manager was male and, for a time, there was a man in charge of the cutting room. The firm attracted employees from the Potteries as well as Leek "At one time they had five buses coming in from the Potteries - different areas - Longton , Sneyd Green, I seem to remember - Brown Edge - bringing girls in."

The clothes made in the Lux Lux factories in Leek went to many foreign markets. "We sold all over the world, really. We sold quite a lot to Saudi Arabia, I seem to remember at one point. We were doing quite well there. But yes, we sold a lot all over the place." The staple buyers were British chain stores such as Littlewoods and Marks and Spencer, but not Harrods. "They thought we weren't good enough, I suppose or something. I think they thought we weren't expensive enough actually. We weren't top-of -the-range. We weren't as expensive as Janet Raeger - and Charnos were a bit dearer than us. But we were middle of the range, really."

After a long career at Lux Lux, as already noted, Rowena was made redundant as were many others of long service to the company. She then had a succession of different jobs. "When I was made redundant from Lux Lux I was approached by Slimma and I went to work in their Technical Department, as they called it. They didn't call it the Design Department. I was a dogsbody. I mean I was making patterns, sorting samples, cutting samples and things like that. I was there for six months. Now, they were always having policy changes, and after six months they had a 'get rid of Rowena' policy change. So, I was a bit upset at being made redundant so soon and Peter Kirkland took pity on me and said, "Well, there is a job you can do, if you like, it's in the Returns Department. So, I said, 'What do I have to do?' and he said, 'Open parcels'. Well, I love opening parcels so I said, 'Oh, lovely'."

"Anyway, this job turned out to be in Nelson Street, five minutes walk from home and, oh, I loved it. I loved that job. You got these wonderful letters, written on formal notepaper -

Dear So and So,

I beg to inform you - you've sent me 3 size 16s instead of a 14, an 18 and a 12 . Would you replace them immediately ...

You visualize Rackham's, you know, somewhere. And then you got these others on a bit of shorthand paper -

Would you mind ... Could you possibly ...

only places like some little shop in Leek, y'know. And then, of course, you had the -

I got it... She's only worn them once ...

She must've put them on for six weeks and never taken them off, and that's all I'll say."

"But, anyway, I was there for six months. Then I was offered a job at Halle Models which was part-time and permanent. So I thought, well, I'd better take it, y'know, 'cos this other one was only temporary. So that's when I went to Halle Models."

This firm made nightwear for ladies and children's clothes. "And there were eight of us in this big Design Department who had all worked at Lux Lux before. So big reunion so far as I was concerned. I was there for two years and then they offered me full-time 'cos they thought I'd go and I said, 'No. I'll take it'. So I stayed on and then at the end of two years I was made redundant and so I left there."

Recollecting the manner of announcing redundancies at different times, Rowena says, "The Halle Models one, I was fuming because the girl who had actually been a trainee at Lux Lux with me, not my trainee but a trainee, came and stood over me and said, 'I've been told to show you off the premises'. So I said, 'Well, I wouldn't have done anything but I bloody well feel like it now'." In practice, Rowena admits that "by then, when we were being made redundant the process was pretty well ironed out. The government had laid down by this time what redundancy should be and what you were supposed to get and there wasn't - nothing you could argue about in any way."

After Halle Models "I was at home for a bit and feeling rather guilty, and then I saw an advertisement for a bridal wear firm who wanted a patternmaker one day a week. So, I worked with them for a while. Actually that was quite an intriguing job because I'd never been so cold in my life. We were working in a room in the old Brough's Mill - huge room, with one oil heater in the middle of the room. It was absolutely perishing. And the first day that I was there, I was making this pattern and I looked down the side of the room at this rack of fabric - and it had got all the bridal wear things at one end. And a bit farther on it had got big rolls of string vest material in red and green and blue and I was thinking, 'Oh, what on earth's that for? Wedding dresses?' And then there was a big roll of - remember Harold Wilson's Gannex mac? Like that. And a big roll of quilting. I thought, well, it can't be wedding dresses. So I asked them what they were and she said, 'Oh, we make horse blankets as well! Which they did on the same machines as they made wedding dresses. Just amazing!'

"Anyway, the horse blanket side got into trouble and that meant I was out of a job again. So I thought, right, that's it. So I didn't work after that."

A lengthy working life followed by a what is for Rowena a very active retirement leads to reflections on change. The virtual disappearance of textile industries from Leek has led to change in the life of the town, but by no means all the alterations can be blamed on the loss of the mills. "Well, yes, I suppose it has changed but I don't know whether that's anything to do with the mills, really. I mean there used to be a time when we had an hour for lunch. And Wednesday used to be absolutely chaotic round about lunchtime because everybody flew up to town to go round the market and all this sort of thing. And then, what happened was, the girls went and said, 'Could they do without an afternoon tea break and finish quarter of an hour earlier in the afternoon?' And something was mentioned about shorter lunch-time, and it was my boss, Mr. Wood, actually, who said, 'Hang on girls. If you do without your afternoon tea break and you cut your lunch down to half an hour you can finish at Friday lunch time'. And so, of course, everybody jumped at that and that's what we did. And so, from then on there really wasn't time for girls to come up into the town in the lunch hour. I mean, they did, occasionally, but there really wasn't time to do it."

Interviewed and transcribed by Trevor Siggers, edited by Paul Anderton

Above: A Lux Lux garment displayed in all its glory.

Above right: a Lux Lux magazine illustrattion.

below right: Wardle & Davenport used this way of advertising its ladies underwear in the 1920's

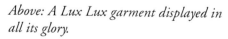

Above

One of the many forms of machining done at Lux Lux

Right

A Lux Lux model demonstrating another of the wide range of nightwear made by the firm

James Bowyer
interviewed November 1987

O Bowyer. He considered that both the type of labour management and nepotism tended to stifle innovation and creative enthusiasm, though the system did offer lifelong job security for those content with their work-place role in the hierarchy of family-run businesses. James loved the challenge of new American machines and took himself to more progressive environments in the factories of Leicester and Nottingham. His experience also spanned the change from shaft and belt-driven mills powered by steam, and locally generated direct current electricity, through to the free standing machines of the post-Depression and post-war (1945) industry.

James Bowyer was born in Leek in 1902 and worked as fitter/maintenance engineer and electrician, first in an established family mill firm, then moved into new forms of textile manufacturing during the 1920s. "We lived in Langford Street, but I was born in Gladstone Street. We moved to Langford Street, eventually - it was a closed street. I don't think it was a closed street when we went there, but it was a closed street until I think I should be ten. I went to West Street School and then I went to a school ... behind the Nicholson Institute. It was called the Leek High School at that time. I went there for a year. I went there after I was fourteen."

He doesn't remember much about his father who died leaving James an only child to be brought up by his mother. There was no possibility of taking up an apprenticeship, James Bowyer explained, because the First World War temporarily closed down that form of beginning work and he stayed at school beyond the age of going into a silk mill on a half-time basis. In fact, he obtained a Certificate in Physics at the High School and

had ambitions for a career in engineering. " I intended, all the time, to go in for engineering - mechanical engineering - and, of course, when I saw the idea of electrical engineering coming into it I thought I'd go into that - but when it come to house wiring - no, I'm not having that."

His first job, lasting about a year, was in a business run by a Mr Hardy, in Stanley Street,. "Well, Hardy was actually a wireman. It was at the time when everything was being altered in Leek. The electrical industry was not developed and houses were done in what was known as 'capping and casing' and that sort of thing and it was house work - wiring houses and that sort of thing. There was no future in that - only as a 'wireman'. I went assisting one of the wiremen outside, you see, before I decided I'd had enough of it. When I left Hardy's I went to Wardle and Davenport's as an assistant electrical engineer."

Telephone 179

GEO. A. HARDY

LIGHTING & GENERAL
ELECTRICAL ENGINEER

Extensive stocks of
SHADES, ELECTRIC FIRES, HEATERS, COOKERS,
DOMESTIC AND LABOUR-SAVING DEVICES

The House for Everything Electrical

OFFICIAL REGISTERED CONTRACTOR TO THE LEEK U.D.C.

You are invited to visit my show rooms without obligation to purchase

CHURCH STREET, LEEK

James Bowyer started going to night school at Leek Technical College during his spell with Hardy's. "I think I did two nights a week. One night was machine drawing, I can remember that, and the other night was in the lab - various experiments. Barents, who was then manager of the Churnet Valley Engineering Company, ... took the machine drawing class. I'm trying to think because I confuse the school teachers that I knew." Two of those were at the High School. "One was Vinen, his brother was the librarian in Leek. And the other, I think, was named Trafford. I'm not sure about that." At Wardle & Davenport's James had plenty of opportunities to learn. "They'd got a generator ... 800 horse-power triple expansion steam engine and a generator on it and it was my job

... when it was started up, to go on the switch board to keep the voltage and the amperage standard while they switched on at different parts of the factory. Get that settled down and then I did whatever job was going - if it was installing a motor or anything like that." The engine and generator were in Big Mill as most people in Leek called it, overlooking Mill Street. But the power was for another part of the firm's premises. "The power went over to

Maintenance work on the Belle Vue site kept James fully occupied. " Well, as I remember, years ago there was two long tables and there was 'ironers' on there. And electric irons in those days were not like they are today. I'd got plenty on to keep these two tables going of irons. Any spare time I'd got I'd always got a lead burnt on these irons and that sort of thing. You see they were plugged in these things - I dare say you've seen them - they're

Wardle & Davenport's winding room in the 1930s with women operating belt driven machinery

the new factory on Belle Vue and we shared it with the electricity company - the change over switch - and we could change over from the 'Town Supply' on to our own. Now this was 'DC' (direct current). Now, if you know anything about electricity you'd realise that you can do more switching over with 'DC' than you can with 'AC' (alternating current), but, of course, by the time it was converted I'd changed from that job. I did it so long and then I went for engineering experience from then on."

plugged in to a centre point. It's a long lead - girls were working either side. Nowadays it'd be different. They had this stuff on blankets and steam heat." The Belle Vue factory was very new and lit as well as powered by electricity, in contrast with Big Mill, then still using gas for lighting. There was a variety of electrically-driven machinery, including sewing machines. Repairing motors was something James often had to do but he wasn't expected to tackle production machinery. "The war had just finished then and I remember this - the main thing about this job - they were making artificial silk coats in those days at Wardle and Davenport's. They were all over the country these silk coats were, in quite a big way. And then they had ... various sorts of knitting circular machines and flat machines and cut-out stuff and that sort of thing. I didn't have much to do with them, you see."

After some two or three years James moved on. "I went to Churnet Valley Engineering Company which was lower down on Newcastle Road. I don't think it's there now. It was a plant that was put down during the war and it had a foundry and everything. It was a complete unit. And after the war it went a bit down-hill They had to take all sorts of things. I don't suppose you've seen the petrol pumps where there was a round casing ... push the casing round and inside it was a pump. Well, we made those - hand pump - you pumped it up. And we did small stuff as well, like work tables for garages. They tried it out. It was the originator of this grease system that they have today, but they had a little pump fastened on which you worked with your hand to pump. So it necessitated two blokes. One to hold the pipe on, the other to turn the grease in. But we made a few of those. We didn't know what they were for, actually. ... And then we did a six and a half-inch centre lathe which was known as 'The Churnet Lathe', and they went all over the world, they did. So we built some of those and, in due course, it's amazing how you gravitate. I gravitated from there back into the textile trade to install some hosiery machines which were coming in then. So I got into the hosiery trade. That's where I wanted to be."

"I went with a firm known as Lilley, Bull & Sons on Buxton Road. They built a new factory on Buxton Road. They were taking some new plant in." The hosiery machines James Bowyer installed on the site of what later became Bode's garage, came from Stibbe's in Leicester. "A man came from the works in Leicester and I became his assistant. I wanted to learn his job. So I learned his job. ... Stibbe's were agents for the Wildman machine which we were putting in. Wildman was, of course, a firm in America. At that time it were

all American machinery coming in. Wardle and Davenport's had got some - what they called Maxims - and this firm was bringing in Wildmans. ... Actually the chap from Leicester had a nice little holiday 'cause I was doing the job. I didn't mind because I wanted to know his job."

"Leek was feeling the Depression then, but it hadn't felt it in the hosiery trade. You see the hosiery trade was just coming into being - into its own." New circular knitting-machines for seamless artificial and real silk stockings changed the nature of the hosiery trade, and James Bowyer saw a bright future. "And I was a seamless man : I never bothered about fully-fashioned I saw that, eventually, people wouldn't - the trade wouldn't cope with everybody wearing 'fully-fashioned'." Not that stockings were everything at Lilley, Bull & Son. "Half the plant there was for ties, knitted ties and scarves. They'd got scarf machines and they'd got circular machines for fabric. And I could handle all of them. I wasn't a bad kid at the time. A lot better then than I am now, of course"

"When we first put seamless machines down a girl would run six on her own, yes. So perhaps they'd have eight. So what have we got, a battery of about 40 - 48 machines. They don't take much room up. It was quite easy for a mechanic to cope with them as long as he knew what he was doing. If he didn't know what he was doing he had 'em round his neck in quick time. The girls couldn't do anything. They'd put a needle in and that sort of thing sometimes, but usually the mechanic was doing the job. So, I would think, at that time, Pretty Polly - Lilley Bull & Son - was operating with about 50 to 60 employees."

James Bowyer had one assistant mechanic. "There were two of us worked there. A chappie - he worked on the sewing machines and lining machines and I coped with the other machines. I wasn't into sewing machines." All were belt-driven from large electric motors, with the sewing machines arranged either side of a long bench, each machine linked to a central shaft bringing power from the motor at the end. Electricity was not generated on site but came from the town supply.

"The chappie I worked directly for was the son", of one of the partners. "He'd been in the RAF in the First World War - it was the Air Force, I think then - and he was also a racing driver. He used to run racing cars, Bugatti and stuff like that, Fraser Nash. And, of course, I had to have a look at these cars you see, and we became quite friends, he and I. We got on very well. I used to do a little job or two for him, y'know, on the side."

It seems that James Bowyer saw a future career at Lilley, Bull & Son, the partners having expensive tastes and, presumably, sufficient capital. "Sid had got a Buick, something like what the Prince of Wales had and Norman Lilley, the son of Lilley, he'd got a Morris Oxford which then was something - you see. Edgar Bull, he'd got a car and I got a motor-bike. In fact, everybody was doing all right, but ... ." Things didn't go as James Bowyer planned. A friend of one of the partners came in to oversee the business and James Bowyer felt he was pushed aside. "Now, my intention was that I was going to run this joint as the engineer and I'd worked hard and worked up to it. I'd put hours and hours in at night when I should have been in bed. But in comes this chap who knew nothing about the trade", and so, in 1927, James left Leek. "So anyway, I went off to Leicester. I'd had enough of it and I went off to Leicester. I told them, I said I'd finished. So I got on my motor-bike and I went off to Stibbe's." "I walked into Stibbes and told them who I was and they soon sorted it out. They'd sent the machines there and it was only a matter of going - 'Yes, yes, when can you start?' I just walked in and said I was accustomed to Wildman's single-headers and the lot and that was it."

This Leicester firm of G. Stibbe did not manufacture machines, it was a specialised importer and installer of American textile machinery, and not a complex industrial concern such as Wardle and Davenport or Brough, Nicholson and Hall. It suited James

Bowyer, therefore, because he had doubts about the kind of career he could have had if he had remained in Leek in their employ. "I'd got a suspicion, I had, that this was to be preferred to going into the big companies which were - the jobs were handed down - well, it was different. I mean, Wardle and Davenport's was so much so that they made their own packing cases to send out. They'd got a joiners' shop, y'know, making packing cases. Well, you can imagine that a tradesman goes into a place like that and he finishes up making packing cases all his life." James Bowyer made the same point a different way. "If you were going to do anything in Leek you'd got to be in the band."

James Bowyer admitted that he was a bit of a rebel and did not find workplaces in Leek to his liking. Family firms could stifle talent as well as provide a comfortable environment for the unambitious. In fact, during a career working in a variety of firms over a wide area he reckoned that he met or heard of Leek men in textile businesses in Nottingham, Leicester, Edmonton in Canada, and in South Africa too, who had left to fulfil aspirations never likely to be satisfied in their home town. "Wherever you go there was a Leek man. They hadn't gone because they wanted to go. They'd gone because the job wasn't worth having, y'see."

Interviewed by Paul Anderton, transcribed by Trevor Siggers and edited by Paul Anderton

"Three-Knots"

REGISTERED TRADE MARK

Hosiery and Underwear of Quality

Janice Brassington

a report of an interview with Rowena Lovatt

*J*anice Brassington's fifteenth birthday was in the middle of the week, but she still started at Job White's mill on her birthday at 7.45am to 6.00pm. On this first morning, she was sent into the 'Bear Pit', which was through the knitting room and down some steps which were like the companionway of a ship and so steep that it was difficult to go down forwards. It had no windows because it was below ground. There were toilets down there, and a little room where they could boil water to make the tea which the girls took there themselves. Doris Swarbrook taught Janice how to make babies' bonnets. This entailed overlocking a piece of 'fleece' leaving three and three-quarter inches open for the baby's neck, and the wire 'grip' at the back was then gathered up and a bobble sewn on top. For her overlocking job Janice was paid four pence farthing, (about 2p) per dozen, which meant that she could earn £8.00 in a good week. The time-wage was only £4.10s.0d, (£4.50), but not bad for 1956. At one point they were short of work so the Union negotiated that in one week they should have Monday and Tuesday off and the following week Thursday and Friday.

Janice thought that this was a great idea and was looking forward to having some time at home, but all those under seventeen had to work by law. The snag was that the management wouldn't put the electricity on, so they just sat at the top of the Bear Pit stairs doing nothing, and after two weeks she gave in her notice.

Then came Clowes & Roberts, where Janice was paid 6d (3p) for making jumpers and this meant that her wage fell to £2.15s.0d (£2.75) a week. Not surprisingly when she heard that White's were busy again she went back, but only lasted from April till

February, then she gave her notice in again and went to work on the biscuit counter at Woolworth's. At seventeen and a half she married and spent the next nine years at home with her children.

Then she went back to White's again. This time she went up the spiral stairs to work on making babies' bootees, an enormously fiddly job working with very small pieces of fleece. So she left again and went to Clowes & Roberts where she stayed for eleven years until they got into financial difficulties. She transferred to Langford Street, but the wages went down and the facilities were not good. There was no canteen and the girls sat at their 'part' to eat their food. Only boiled water was provided.

So, after a short spell at Lux Lux, doing side seams and working for the first time on a 'team', Janice went to Halle Models where she remained for the next fourteen years, starting as an overlocker. Then an order came in which had some flatlocking on it, and Don Bagshaw, the mechanic, asked her to have a go and she ended up doing the whole order herself. This led to her becoming a 'floater' at £30.00 more than time-wage. She worked on any team

HALLE MODELS (LEEK) LTD. Lingerie

doing the work of any girl who was missing. She enjoyed this because there was something different nearly every day and the time went by quickly.

But time went by even quicker when, after two years, she was moved to the design department where her skills on all the machines in the factory were much in demand. Perhaps the most difficult thing for a sample-hand to do is to tell the designer that what she wants can't be made by mass-production methods. As a rule, this did not happen with designers who had spent time on machines and who, therefore, had the experience to know what was possible, but others who had only been to College and had no experience of piece-work tended to design things without much thought as to the feasibility of making a garment on industrial machines at high speed. Obviously, if insufficient money has been allowed for the time taken to make something up due to the difficulty involved, then the garment will only be produced at a loss. If a sample hand didn't mention this problem at the time, then later the designer would turn round and say, 'Janice never said it was difficult'! Then again, some designers would refuse to believe it couldn't be done, and it was not unusual for some sample-hands to have a 'black book' with their opinions written in it and witnessed by others!

Sadly, it was just such a disagreement as this that led to Janice walking out of Halle Models and ending her working life in the rag trade

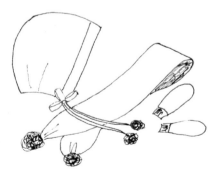

John Newall

interviewed November 2005

*P*eople who spent a lifetime working in Leek's textile trades frequently started, immediately on leaving school, from a family connection. John Newall's father was joint-managing director of A.J.Worthington & Co. with a factory on Portland Street. "My father wanted me to get an idea of the textile industry ... and I wanted to as well because I didn't really know what I wanted to do. And so, before I was called up for my National Service, I went to work at William Frost's in Macclesfield for a year, from September 1951 until July 1952 and, also, attended Macclesfield Technical College at the same time to get some kind of grounding in textile technology." This was arranged through the chairman of Worthington's, William Wadsworth, who was also the managing director of the Macclesfield firm.

John Newall easily recalls the autocratic style of William Wadsworth and "the princely sum of £1.00 per week which was handed to me on Friday afternoon, with considerable ceremony, by the cashier, Mr Berry, who had a polished light-pine coloured head, and always wore a stiff collar and bow-tie". Training "consisted of 'sitting with Nellie' and I attended Macclesfield Technical College two or three mornings and several evenings each week". He had digs with a Mrs. Fletcher, bed and board at £3.00 per week. "This was my introduction to silk and I will never forget the sense of wonder which it gave me. It was so beautiful. It had a slightly crisp feel, like human hair, and a marvellous lustrous sheen".

Two years in the army didn't alter John Newall's career intentions, though his father's death shortly before John's return to Leek perhaps strengthened the impulse to continue in the family tradition. "What happened was that I came out of the Army at the end of August 1954 but my father, in the meantime, had died at the end of March '54. And so I felt, really, as an only son, and with my father's connection with the business that it was almost my duty to go and work at the family firm, if

you like, Worthington's, and so I started off as a trainee at Worthington's virtually straightaway ... and, as it happened, I found it enjoyable and interesting and so my career developed from there."

"I was eleven years at Worthington's altogether and I spent time in each of the firm's departments. Worthington's was one of the, if you like, old-fashioned, traditional-type of Leek companies, like Brough, Nicholson & Hall, Wardle and Davenport, Job White, and others, in that it produced a very wide range of different types of textiles. It produced sewing tread; braids and trimmings; Sander and Graff trimmings; warp-knitted fabrics; circular-knitted fabrics; and had its own dye-house. And, so really, it was quite - Oh, it also had narrow fabric weaving as well. So, it was very diverse."

"In the end, I finished up in the sewing-thread department of Worthington's. The manager was a chap called Roland Lyon and I worked with Roland for several years and then I was made a director of the company."

John Newall started out in 1954 in "the Sander and Graff trimming section which, at that time, was housed in Queen Mill, on the right-hand side of Queen Street - the part that's now been turned into apartments." The machines "are officially called 'trimming looms' and they rely upon a technique which is half-way between knitting and weaving. A bed of needles knits a chain stitch longitudinally along the fabric and then carriers carry threads across this row of stitches which are then locked in by the next row of stitches and so produces a fabric... a narrow fabric. Infinite huge versatility these machines had. Sander

the director in charge of the Sander and Graff department was a man called Arthur Pace, whose father was Jerry Pace who was very well-known in Leek cricketing circles in the latter part of the nineteenth and early twentieth centuries. And Arthur Pace was an absolute wizard with these machines. He could do anything with them."

There were dozens of these machines at work at any one time, crowded together, all operated by women. The finished narrow fabrics were also inspected for faults in the same room, wound on to cards of specific sizes, and boxed and made ready for transporting to clothing manufacturers or wholesale warehouses. "There was a tremendous buzz of activity and there was always, if you like, a cheerful hum going on. It was a cheerful sort of place to work in ... Oh, it wasn't

A. J. Worthington's mill on both sides of Queen Street

and Graff were a German company, based in Chemnitz, in what was East Germany, and they were copied - their idea was copied - by various other companies, but they always remained the kind of standard by which all other manufacturers were judged. And Sander and Graff was as synonymous with trimming looms as Frigidaire is with refrigerators or Hoover with cleaners."

"Well, what I did - I fetched and carried. I mostly helped the fettlers (the mechanics) setting up new patterns on the machines and that taught me the intricate workings of the machines and the patterning possibilities that came from them. And, I should mention that

a deafening noise at all. It was a kind of gentle clash, clash, clash noise, but not like a braid department or a spinning room or, shall we say, a broad-loom weaving plant." John remembers there was plenty of opportunity for chat and gossip. He had always known something of what the atmosphere of factory work was like. "Many of the older operators knew me since I was a small child because my father used to take me to the factory, and that kind of thing."

Every section of the trade had its own intricacies and specialities, "but I think, in the end, the department which I finished up in, namely the threads department, was the one which determined my future career in that I specialised in sewing thread from then on until I finished work. We're talking about sewing thread for industrial purposes not for domestic purposes. You see, originally Worthington's, like Anthony Ward and other Leek companies, produced pure silk thread for the tailoring trade and that was still running when I first started in the industry. It was much smaller than it had been but, nevertheless, it was still there and they were still supplying tailoring companies and also companies making ecclesiastical vestments and things like that with pure silk threads. But, from the early part of the war - the Second World War - nylon had started to be used ... and when I went to Frost's in 1951, Frost's was still absolutely, fully engaged in the production of silk yarns: in their case, not for sewing thread but for weaving and knitting and so on, stocking manufacture and everything like that. By the time I came out of the Army in 1954, silk had got the skids under it. Nylon and Polyester were coming in tremendously rapidly and the whole industry went through a huge convulsive revolution which brought an end to the reign of silk, the so called 'Queen of Fibres'. Worthington's still produced silk sewing thread in small quantities but the huge majority of its production was going for industrial purposes and was made of nylon and polyester. The original fibre was extruded into continuous filament form by such companies as Courtauld's, British Nylon Spinners, ICI, and so on. And we bought the yarn which had almost no twist in it at all and we twisted it; built it up into different thicknesses; dyed it; lubricated it; wound it on to sales package and so on."

The basic operation in the manufacture of sewing threads from single filament silk and artificial fibres is the imparting of twist. The correct term, as John Newall explained, is 'throwing'. The term 'spinning' is more correctly applied to short-fibred textiles, such as wool and cotton - and 'waste silk'. This, as the name implies, is a mass of short filaments accidentally created during 'throwing'.

"Well, the main outlets for Worthington's thread was for the parachute and allied industries which was a continuation from what the company had done during the Second World War. But, also, at that time, Worthington's supplied a lot of synthetic thread for sewing fertilizer sacks. Fertilizer sacks had been sewn with cotton thread and, apparently, the story goes that several hundred tons of fertilizer was delivered by Fison's, or one of the large companies, and was put on the dockside of a port in Cyprus and when they came to have a look at it several months later the sacks had disintegrated into a great big heap of fertilizer, and they realised that they had got to do something about the sewing thread. And so, I don't know how, Worthington's got in touch with such companies as Fison's, but they developed a sewing thread which did the purpose very well indeed. And so, Worthington's not only supplied the fertilizer manufacturers who were putting the fertilizer into the bags, they also supplied the bag manufacturers like Bowwater's, Medway Paper Sacks, Abertay Paper Sacks, and so on, who sewed across the bottom of the sack during the sack's production."

Not that Worthington's had much by way of a research and development section. Specialist chemists, for example, were not employed. Trial fibres were only subject to physical tests. "It was purely physical and the testing was done, really, by the customers. You would work with the customer and try to develop something that the customer thought was practical and useful and build up on that. But the customer never demanded any kind of patent from it, or any rights from it. It was just one of those things, if you could develop it with the customer first, then he would probably derive benefit from that before you started to expand its use into other parts of industry. An example of that was when Worthington's were in at the very early days at the production of car seat belts; and one of the original manufacturers of car seat belts was a firm called Britax, and Worthington's worked very closely with them to develop suitable sewing threads to withstand the strain of accidents."

Responsibility for seeking new customers as well as devising new products was left with the production managers. There was no marketing department. "Worthington's was highly compartmentalised or departmentalised, and in sewing-thread I worked with Roland Lyon on developing new products. In the braid department it would be Noel Bowcock and Ron Foster who did it, and so on. And the man who probably had the best all-seeing eye, certainly had the best all-seeing eye after my father died, was Harry Millward. And Harry Millward was a sewing thread specialist really, but he had a broad mind and could see potential in all kinds of different directions. And so, he would encourage individual departments to develop their own ideas and run with them."

John Newall's pattern of work came to include more travelling, though he has no clear memory of how this gradually evolved within the British domestic market. "My first foreign journey was to Holland and Belgium in the spring of 1958 and that really started me off on what was perhaps my main theme and that was the development of the export business. And that remained a very strong theme throughout my career."

When asked about how he researched the market for exports John Newall replied, "That's a very difficult question to answer because what happened was we never ever found one single, reliable, long-term distributor through using the various agencies which were available to companies to employ. For example, shall we say, the Department - as it is now - the Department of Trade and Industry or anything like that. We never found a single agent or distributor that

way. It all came by word of mouth. And our starting pointing in Europe was our agent-distributor in Switzerland. He recommended a company in Holland to us. They recommended a company in Germany. The people in Holland recommended somebody in France who recommended somebody in Belgium. And those were by far the most successful contacts we made and it went step by step over quite a number of years."

Eleven years at Worthington's and appointment as a company director gave John Newall a firm base in Leek's textile trade, but perhaps a feeling that there was more that could be done. He denies that he attracted the attention of the managing director of Anthony Ward & Co., Sam Bradshaw, because of interest in export markets, but John was nevertheless invited to move to Ward's.

"Well, shortly, I think it was only within two years of my becoming a director, I was approached by the managing director of Anthony Ward, Sam Bradshaw, and he asked me if I would like to join his company. And I suppose, really, at that time I was thirty and I thought that I wanted to spread my own wings in my own way. And so, I left Worthington's and joined Anthony Ward as sales director in 1965." Bradshaw had been an officer in the Colonial Service and married John Ward's daughter, Clover. The firm occupied Albion Mill at the top of King Street which the first Anthony Ward had built in the 1820s.

Albion Mill in June 1988 when just over one hundred and sixty years old

John Newall was asked whether many firms in Leek in the early 1960s actively developed export markets. "I would say - largely not. Obviously, there were exceptions but I would say largely not." Personally, John was helped in looking for European outlets by his skill in languages. French was first picked up at school alongside German, but it was National Service which gave him his best opportunity for foreign language practice. "Well, it's curious really because I studied French and German at school and when I went to the Army I joined the Intelligence Corps and was sent to Germany as a member of an organisation called the British Intelligence Interpreters' Pool and we were busy on intelligence gathering operations which involved my interviewing or translating interviews with Germans. And this imprinted German on my mind very strongly indeed. Then, some years later, really, I got back into French again and that developed or redeveloped itself very quickly. And so the two languages became essential tools to me in later years not as, shall we say, 1958 when I first started going abroad but it gradually grew during the 1960s after I joined Ward's."

As to the business of other firms, "I just think they felt satisfied with their UK markets - with what they were familiar - because it was still, at that time, late 1950s early 1960s ... we were still in almost a 1920s - 1930s sales and purchasing pattern. The wholesale warehouses in the big cities like London, Manchester, Glasgow, Leeds and so on, were still very powerful. The chain stores had not really got going in the same sense. Obviously, there was Marks & Spencer, British Home Stores and Littlewoods but they were not really anything like as powerful at that time as they became."

In other words, in the immediate post-war period the wholesalers of fabrics and cloth supplying the dress manufacturing trades re-asserted their traditional role and shaped the nature of production. The war, however, had necessarily affected textile firms and Worthington's exemplified how new opportunities were there for the taking. "Well, you see, really, Worthington's position derived from a bit of inspiration of my father's in the 1930s because, one day, a business friend of his, knowing that my father was a braiding expert, dangled a piece of braided material in front of him and said, 'This is what you should be in, Harry'. And he said, 'What's that?' He said, 'Parachute cord'. 'Oh yes?' This was 1937 and

so my father set about getting Worthington's into, if you like, a pole position, before the outbreak of hostilities in September 1939, whereby Worthington's produced sewing thread for parachute manufacture, parachute cords and things called periphery tapes which went round the edge, the skirt of the parachute which, at that time, was circular rather than the oblong things you see now. And these periphery tapes were made on Sander and Graff trimming looms. So that was another part of Worthington's business which was absolutely engaged in industrial output. And it was a tremendous strength of Worthington's all the way through the War. And so, Worthington's had got themselves into satisfying industrial demands and accustomed to the idea of going for industrial demands through their experience in the war and then started profiting by, for example, the supply of threads for fertilizer sack sewing. That was something totally outside the usual Leek experience or market."

John Newall suggested that it was also the re-organisation of manufacturing assets to meet war requirements that assisted Worthington's. "What happened was that companies, as I understand it, were concentrated. In other words, obviously, there wasn't the manpower or womanpower to keep all production going and so a number of firms were put into a kind of suspended animation. I can't tell you which ones in Leek were put into suspended animation or were told to work to the instructions of other companies like Worthington's who had an inside track to the Ministry of Aviation, parachute manufacturers and so on. I can't really tell you, but that's what happened in effect. And so Worthington's were in a very strong position at the end of the War to move in an industrial direction."

Parachute manufacture was labour-intensive. "In the braid department it was a bit odd because in the parachute cord-making section the machine operators were all women but in the, if you like, 'fancy trimmings' side making all kinds of zigzag, what you call rickrack trimmings/braids and so on, they were mostly men and I never knew why that should be. But, for example, in the braid department in the parachute section one of the curious things about the parachute cord production was that every inch of every cord was examined by hand before it was wrapped up into balls, to send to the parachute manufacturers, to see whether there were any lumps - uneven places which could provide a weak place in the cord. So imagine, the hundreds and hundreds of thousands of miles of parachute cord, every single one passed through the hands, the fingers, of a trained female operator/inspector."

At the time he worked for the firm, Worthington's employed about 250-260 people in its five manufacturing departments. The greater majority were women. "In the sewing thread department all the operators were women. Of course, at the time, one used to have twelve-hour shifts. Until the idea of the eight-hour shifts came in you did have twelve-hour shifts and, of course, if they were night shifts they were always men. That's how it divided itself." Each department had its own specialist mechanics and a foreman and deputy foreman, invariably men, but the office was staffed largely by women. There were works electricians and a joiner; a fitting shop and a joiner's shop, but no box-making shop.

Businesses in Leek's textile trades varied considerably in size and in complexity. Each had a tendency to focus on certain processes or products, and they were both complementary and in competition. They could give help to each other on occasions: they could be very secretive. "I would say that, fundamentally, they kept themselves very much to themselves. Although, of course, there was a Leek Manufacturers' and Dyers' Association and they used to meet regularly, and I, myself, often attended meetings not infrequently. But I think they all regarded each other with reserve. Perhaps one should say that, of course, in Leek there were several different basic sections. There was, shall we say, fabric dyeing as represented by Premier Dyeing Company, Joshua Wardle and Sir T. & A. Wardle; the yarn dyers such as William Tatton, Clewes and so on, Brassey and others; and then there were the mixed companies such as Worthington's, Milner's, Brough, Nicholson & Hall, and Wardle & Davenport, and Davenport Adams; and then there were the light clothing manufacturers such as Lux Lux and Earle's".

One of the principal items for the manufacturers to discuss in their Association was wage-rates. "The problem for the Leek industry, as a whole, was that when it was negotiating wage-rates the various sections of Leek industry had quite different ideas as to what would constitute what was, shall we say, a reasonable increase in wages from one year to the next. Because, clearly, the labour-intensive companies such as the light clothing manufacturers were far more sensitive to an increase of one percent in the wage rate, in other words, giving them, shall we say, six and a half percent instead of five and a half percent than people which were more capital-intensive such as the sewing thread manufacturers."

Decisions on wages were to some extent simplified by the existence of only one union across the whole range of workers employed in the industry. Relationships between union and employers were matters of significance and, in John Newall's view, "They were quite good. The person who I remember the most about is the union secretary was a chap called Herbert Lyle and Herbert was union secretary for many years and he was a bluff, cheerful character but he had, I think - my personal opinion - he had a very good heart and he was a reasonable sort of chap and, although manufacturers being manufacturers they always complain about the union, in fact, generally speaking there was a pretty amicable arrangement or amicable atmosphere between the manufacturers and the union."

In the higher ranks of management there had been a traditional "informal agreement between the manufacturers right up to the outbreak of the Second World War whereby you didn't 'poach' other people's key workers or executives. And, I won't go into the detail because - because it is personal to one or two people. But I did know of one instance where a transfer from one company to another was stopped by a kind of behind-the-scenes deal between the two manufacturers concerned. This was before the War. Now then, obviously, during the War, because of the absence of so many thousands of people on Service, of course, this became very much weaker. And, really, in the 1950s and 1960s, I'm not conscious of the idea that there was a problem about moving from one company to another. After all, I moved from Worthington's to a partial competitor, namely Ward's. Ward's only competed with Worthington's on part of Worthington's sewing thread production. It wasn't even a head-to-head over the whole range of sewing threads and, certainly, sewing thread was only one part of Worthington's total production. It really didn't impinge on Worthington's very hard at all."

Worthington's was not the only Leek manufacturing concern which retained the character of a family firm even after becoming a public company - in this case, in January 1954. Ward & Co. was very much a family business when John Newall joined. It too, eventually, followed the path of others. "In 1987 Ward's was taken over by Oxley Threads (of Ashton-under-Lyne) ... and I joined Oxley's in charge of their export sales and also special assignments. Then Oxley's decided, really quite rightly, that they'd got two of everything - two spinning plants; two administrations; two stocks; and so it made sense, unfortunately, to close Anthony Ward down because, in any case, Oxley's was about six times as large as Anthony Ward. And I was with them for seven years until I retired at the age of sixty".

Reflecting on the changes in Leek's textile trades since the early 1950s John Newall makes a sharp distinction between the older thread-making and dress-trimmings businesses on one side and light-clothing manufacturers on the other. This was not only in sensitivity to wage-rate changes but also in labour turnover, with a higher rate affecting the clothing makers. He also looks back on what maybe called the short-sightedness of many of the

long-established firms. In fact, they were "complacent" and, to some extent, this explains their disappearance. "Obviously, there are still companies in the textile sector in general, including textile engineering and so on, in the Leek area who are still doing well: who have developed their export markets. You see the problem was that people did think that their quite prosperous home market would continue for ever. I felt in my bones that the future of our companies rested in exports and, in fact, that's been borne out over the long term. The problem is, of course, that what I considered to be our export markets, shall we say like Germany and France, and Italy and Portugal, have now disappeared because those markets have been transplanted to the Far East ... people complain now about job losses in Leek. The real job losses, the big job losses in Leek were 30 years ago, 25 years ago. That's when the real damage was done."

Finally, challenged to react to the view that on the factory and mill floors in the sewing-thread and braid-making trades those operating the machines in the older businesses found them happy, jolly places, John Newall was cautious. "I wouldn't put it quite as strongly as that but, nevertheless, I felt there was an underlying cheerfulness amongst everybody, really. It wasn't gloom and despondency. It wasn't feeling oppressed or anything like that. Mind you, I'm speaking from a position of privilege and so it's difficult to be absolutely sure about that. But that was the impression I always had. That it was a friendly atmosphere." Did workers feel that they were being looked after by their employers? "Mostly. Once again it's very dangerous to generalise but I think that, in general terms people were fairly happy but I think you'd have to ask somebody who was at the, you know, down below looking up".

Interviewed and edited by Paul Anderton
Recorded and transcribed by Trevor Siggers

Leek's long established manufacture of sewing threads and dress trimmings such as braids and labels won a world-wide reputation. Children's wear and ladies nightdresses using knitted fabrics and artificial fibres became the dominant products in the later twentieth century.

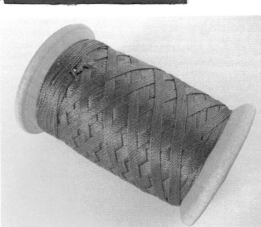

Norah Clarke

interviewed in March 2005

Norah Clarke was born Norah Merriman on the 26 August 1914, "on Ashbourne Rd, across from where the Talbot pub is now. There were stone cottages, about five, along there. My mother lived in one of those. I'd got two sisters and a brother when I was born. We moved to Derby and my mother had a baby there, Nancy. Then we came back to Leek and she had another baby a little while after. I'd got two younger and two older sisters. There were five girls and one brother, but my brother died when he was 22 and my mother died the following year ... my brother died in 1927. Fred died in the October, my mother died the following November. She had him in bed two years with heart trouble ... double leakage in his heart. I was fourteen when my mother died. I was only seven when my father died ... when we lived in Church Street and it broke the home up. My mother got married again and he wouldn't go to work ... he didn't like work I don't think."

Norah went "to the Catholic school down King Street. We lived in Beatty Rd, a new house right up the top of Buxton Rd. In them days ... there was no Prince Street ...it was a tip ... you run down one side, and you run up th'other! Only kids went because they could run down the bank and back up. We walked school every day ... me with a parcel to take to the pawnshop ... as big as myself on a Monday because that was for the rent. And if my mother wanted me she used to just come on th'path and shout, 'Eh lady, I want you go down Ernie Carter's.' I knew Ernie Carter's and all his staff better than I knew them in th'house ... I went

Norah, aged nineteen, at Blackpool on a five-shilling day-trip

that often!" Ernie Carter kept the pawnshop.

Norah had no great aspirations about her future employment. "Only in the mill ... I knew my life was going to be in the mill. As long as I brought money home at the weekend ... that was the only thing that you thought about in them days." When Norah started work her mother was ill in hospital at Hartshill, where she later died. "My grandma had got a job for me at Milner's in Union Street, just above the Majestic [cinema]... she worked there my grandmother did. It was sticking labels on little cops ... ready for the machines to put the cotton on ... sewing thread. When I first went there I did a lot of errands ... a lot of running about. My mother was in hospital and I wasn't interested in the job at all. I was wondering what I was going to do if my mother came home ... what was going to happen ... and eventually ... it was on a Saturday ... we was at Maggie Arthur's ... it was a friend of my mother's and she looked after us when my mother was in hospital. And somebody came and told Maggie that my mother had died. My sister, Gladys, took me to my grandma's and she was so upset about my mother going ... and I was as well. Anyway, the home was broke up ... the funeral happened ... we stood round the table and they sorted us out. Nancy was going with my Auntie Rose ... and Gladys and Eileen were going with my Aunt Nell ... there was only me left ...and nobody wanted me ... so my Aunt Nell took me. So I went with my other two sisters and we stayed there for twelve months ... and it were the happiest twelve months of my life. She lived in Hall Avenue, up on the housing scheme. She'd got two daughters ... and a nephew ... he lived there with his mother. I don't know how she put us up but she did ... me and our Gladys and Eileen slept in one bed in a big double bedroom."

One incident Norah remembers well, and recalls with a chuckle. "My Auntie Rose had fetched me out of work and took me and rigged me up with clothes ... and she also bought me a corset ... I was only fourteen you know. And I couldn't get in this corset ... I couldn't fasten it! I used to have to get our Gladys to come and pull it to for me! We stayed there for twelve months and then Gladys said to my Aunt Nell, 'I'm getting married at Christmas' ... and my Aunt Nell says, 'Well, when you go take these with you' ... that was me and Eileen. Gladys says, 'Well, Eileen's coming with me, I'll take our Norah down to my grandma's'. And my grandma had me, and my grandma taught me how to wash and iron and cook. She lived at the back of the Queen's Head pub ... down the entry. It was only one up and one down. I used to do the cleaning and that. I used to give my grandma five shillings ... she arranged what to do. 'You must give me five shillings [25p], Norah, and I shall take you to Billy Harrison's and get him to get you a nice suit'. So she took me and I had this suit and I had to pay one shilling and six pence [8p] a week off it ... so that was five shillings for my board and one shilling and six pence, and if I wanted my shoes mending that was another six pence [3p], so I had to be very careful as I trod!" Norah recalls her weekly wage at this time was 7s/6d [38p]. I made friends with Kate Hulme ... and that Christmas she bought me a pair of gloves. My mother had died in the November and she said, 'Norah, what do you want for Christmas? Do you want a box of chocolates or a pair of gloves?' 'Ooh,' I said, 'I'll have some gloves please,' and she bought me some fleecy lined gloves."

Norah was soon moved to work as a spooler at Milner's. "He put me on piece-work because I was quick at it ... I got ten shillings." [50p] Norah describes her job as a spooler. "They brought you a tray full of bobbins ... only little

bobbins like that", and she indicated that they were just over one inch tall, the size of a modern reel of cotton. "And you used a machine and you had to put so many rows on one bobbin ... filling the bobbins. And you'd got to measure each one ... and you'd got a knife ... and you had to cut it ... pull the thread through and cut it off. You'd have about 24 on one tray and they'd come and take them as you filled it up. Then they would go into ... where all the boxing was done. It was higher standard than being in the mill ... being in the making-up department." Norah recalls the boss of the room being a Mr. Harrison.

When asked about working hours, Norah replied, "You went from quarter to eight 'till quarter to six," and worked some Saturday mornings, "but not always ... because I remember some Saturday mornings I used to do the cleaning because a lad used to come from Mear's corner. They sold all vegetables and they used to bring grandma's vegetables ... and he used to ask me to go the pictures with him." Norah laughs heartily at the memory! Norah has only vague memories of lunchtime. "I think we took sandwiches. My grandmother always got a dinner for night. What was left on Sunday ... it would last us 'till nearly Thursday!"

"I didn't stay there [Milner's] long. Joyce, who lived with me at my Aunt Nell's, ... she was going to look for another job, and says, 'Come with me Norah. If you get it you'll get more money than where you are.' I shouldn't have gone you know because my grandma had got me that job and my grandma worked there. Anyway I went and got this job. I went Birch's in Britannia Street ... it's flats now. [Brunswick Mill] I did knitting on knitting machines. But being young they put you on all the oldest knitting machines they'd got. It weren't good material ... they knit that sort of wool that they made gloves for the soldiers."

"I had some happy times at Birch's because I was only young. They took us on an outing. We went twice, two years running. The first time we went to Buxton. It was a cricket match. I don't know who were playing cricket like but we were going. And when we got there Norman and Stanley were Birch's sons ... and he brought me ... showed me what there was for tea ... he brought me this menu. There was fresh salmon and salad ... and I thought I'm having that. I'd never had it before ... and we had a lovely tea. We didn't stop watching the cricket. We went for a walk round the fields and having a look up at Buxton ... it was somewhere different. And one of the sons brought me home. I didn't come home with the others on the bus ... I had a lift." Norah laughingly recalls, "because I was only young ... I suppose I thought they're giving me a day out. And then we went to Dovedale and we went across them stones ... stepping stones at Ilam." Norah is unsure whether on that particular occasion they took a picnic or had lunch at the Peveril of the Peak.

Norah is very fond of music, and at Birch's, "I used to sing my head off. He sent me upstairs on another job. He was always messing me about. They could do that because I was only young ... I wasn't married or anything ... I'd got the world in a 'bont'! I'd got no mother and father for t' say anything, so I just did what I was told. I had to go upstairs and a man who worked there says, 'Where's that little wench as sings ... it's like a wot'sit in here since she's gone'. He meant say to there's no fun in this room since she's gone 'cos I used to sing a lot ... always singing ... and I still do!"

Norah has an amusing tale to tell about her time at Birch's and laughs as she talks animatedly. "Nutty Jones used to put me in a bobbin basket and run me all around the room ... got run all round the room ... and all the women used to be shouting at him! Oh I thought Nutty was lovely ... he was handsome! He used to catch hold of me and drop me in one of these baskets ... and run round with me! And I'll tell you another thing that he used to do. If I'd washed my hair and put it in curlers and made myself look nice ... he used to squirt th' oil-can on my hair. He used to say, 'Come near me and I shall squirt this oil-can on yer! Oh, we had some happy times there. But not that the bosses knew about it ... you had to do it when they weren't in. Mr Birch used to come in because we were fooling about. One of the Birch's sons, an older one ... he used to work on one machine and he'd stay on it all morning perhaps ... just go down for a cup of tea ... never used to speak to anybody ... but Stanley did and Norman did. They were alright with us ... was alright with me because I never took any notice of 'em ... I treated 'em same as myself."

Norah recalls mill dances. "It was always in the winter time. We used to go to the Town Hall ... have new dresses. I remember the first dance we went to with Birch's. It was over the Co-op up Ashbourne Rd ... that big room up there."

A metal tag for registering arrival at work

"I went Brough's because my sister worked at Brough's. I was working at Brough's when I got married." Norah married Jack Clarke, a bricklayer. Norah worked on raschel looms at Brough's, and describes the job of working such a loom. "You had to thread them in. You'd have a warp ... bring you a warp and drop it in up here ... and all your threads were stuck on a piece of paper like that. And you'd have to get the threads between your fingers and thread the machine in before you could do anything ... 'cos it was as wide as this house I bet the machine would be! There was a note with the warp telling you what it was ... sometimes it was black silk. If it were black silk it used to give you th'headache ... Ooh it did! But anyway I did alright. Once it was put up there, the two lads went who put you the warp up ... and then you'd have to pull it down ... and would tell how many threads to each hole ... or double your thread. You'd got to work with your head as well as your fingers ... and you'd got be nimble for t' get 'em all in ... get it done as quick as you possibly could to get the machine going. And then you had to go and get a woman for t' come and have a look what you'd done ... if it was all threaded in right before you'd started the machine up. If it wasn't threaded right it would be done wrong. Elijah Handley used to come to me and he'd say, 'They're complaining bitterly, Norah!' I says, 'Why? What have I done now?' 'You've left a thread out in such and such a warp and she's having to run it in.' She could run it in ... it wasn't a waste. I said, 'Well it doesn't matter. I'll watch it next time' ... so I got rid of it like that. And on circular knitting, a bobbin might not be running ... it would be going round and you'd think all your bobbins ... but one of 'em would run off perhaps. And when they come for t' look ... examining your work there'd be a dropped thread ... perhaps all through where it changed ... and you've never noticed it ... that could happen. And then the menders had to pick that up. There were menders there for t' do things like that ... I've bin on mending an' all."

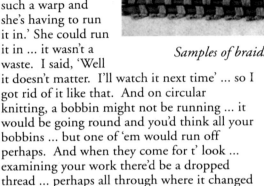

Samples of braids from early 1920s

Some years later Norah went to Milner's in Langford Street. Norah remembers the room there as being "half full of knitting machines. A quarter of it was circular knitting machines, and then a quarter of it was raschel looms, and then the other lot was winding and carding ... putting all the cotton on cards, and there was winding frames and putting labels on." She describes the noisy atmosphere of the mill in Langford Street. "I always thought I'd be deaf, and I am! Ooh! and the noise ... when I went in I thought, 'No, I can't stand this'. It made my head go funny! But I went ... I was on Sander and Graff [machines]. There was like a partition in between this braid tenting and the machinery. I stayed there because I was used to it ... and I got good money there. Sander

and Graff wasn't too bad ... it was a lot more clicking like. No, it wasn't noisy, not like in the braid department. You could put up with it where I worked but you couldn't put up with working in the braid."

"When I worked for Arthur Goodwin at Milner's, I used to do braid on a sewing machine ... cans full of braid ... and you had to keep filling them, machining the two ends together with packing in." This braid would be used as part of the upholstery for armchairs and settees. "I got plenty of money on that ... and then it went a bit slack ... and he says, 'Do a bit o' fringing for me, Norah ... just try it.' Well, I knew how to fringe ... my mother had fringed at work . My mother used to work at Brough's on fringing ... and I used to fetch homework for her ... and you know what they got ... one penny for a hundred knots! So when who's it showed me how to do it ... I could do it. I went along and he says, 'Norah, I'm going to give you a price for that ... you can go on piece-work ... you can earn some money.' So I says, 'Can I take it home?' He says, 'Yes.' So I took it home. I did it at night ... and it was silk fringe, and it was for the Jews in Manchester ... white silk fringe. You did two rows ... you did one row and joined your silks together ... so you'd got a diamond. But it all depends what people wanted ... how many rows of diamonds they wanted. There was a lot of Jews in Manchester then. They put me on piece-work and he give me ever such a good price for it ... that's why I took it home ... and our Pam [Norah's younger daughter] used to help me. We used to sit with the ironing board ... and fasten it all along the ironing board ... because it was long ... you'd got keep taking it off and putting it on again. We used to sit 'till one o'clock in a morning. I made ever such a lot of money at that ... it was grand. It was hard work mind you ... you didn't get anything for nothing ...

never." At Milner's in Langford Street, "They was all very nice. There was another floor higher up ... Mary Yates used to work up there. They did close work. I know a young woman who works up there ... she used to show her underwear off ... Mabel Kirkham ... she was a mannequin for it ... a lovely looking woman."

"When I went working at Davenport's I was on Sander and Graff." This was making "narrow fabrics for putting round the edges of suites and fringing for to put round a table lamp ... same as them bobbles on there," she says, pointing to a lamp. "That's done on Sander and Graff [machines]. There's another thread on the end of them bobbles before it's finished ... there's another thread that goes round. You knit all that in ... on the end of the bobbles there's one thread and that's pulled all out after it's been put on the lamp shade so that the bobbles are loose ... that's how that's done."

"I've bin on fully-fashioned hose ... that was at Wardle and Davenport's. I'd got children growing up then ... Maureen would be twelve or fourteen years old [in the mid-1950s]. I did seaming ... they called it linking. You did the heels ... you put the heels together on a machine ... a big cylinder ... and you had to put the stitches on like that. They was already knit ... the hose were. And you'd have to pick the material up and thread them on and do the heel and down the back of the heel. You had to put the stocking together and then the seamers used to do the seaming, but we did the linking ... that was linking the hose together ... and all fully-fashioned." Mr Agars "was over the hose room ... and we all used to sing, and if we sang a hymn and he liked it he used to ask us to sing it again. He was ever such a nice man ... but we didn't speak very highly of him because he was the boss." Norah relates a story that almost amounted to a women's mutiny. The women thought they should be entitled to a pair of fully-fashioned hose 'on the firm'. "We all went to Mr Agars and asked him ... and he said we couldn't. He said it was our work and it was what we were paid for. But anyway we got them ... we got two pair ... all the women. I think it was through Mr. Davenport ... Tony Davenport ... he was over the mill. I think with us all saying we wanted

them, he give way." Norah remembers the time when the making of fully-fashioned hose moved away from Leek. "They left and went down London. All our knitting machines went ... the ones that did hose ... I don't know why."

Norah remembers being paid on Fridays, and she had a good wage compared to her husband, especially when she worked on Sander and Graff. "I got nearly as much as Jack ... Jack got nothing bricklaying you know ... because if it only looked like rain they sent 'em home. In the early days sometimes your wage was in a can ... the can had a number on ... tipped it out of a can ... but as it advanced it was in a packet." She recalls the daily procedure of clocking in. "You had a card to clock in with ... sometimes one would clock in for another you know ... if you knew she was coming late. But I never asked anybody to do it for me because you wasn't supposed to do it. Our lodgeman ... if he saw you coming he'd close the gate. He'd let you in but you'd lose quarter of an hour because it would be on your clock. They worked on the right side the mill owners did ... that's how the mill owners got their money out of ordinary working people."

Throughout her working life Norah has done many different jobs in Leek's textile mills, operating a range of machinery, each requiring new skills. Most seem to have been learnt by 'watching Nellie'. Norah remembers a woman from whom she learnt some particular techniques. "When I was at Davenport's, Hilda Christie showed me what to do and how to get on. She was very good to me. I was on raschel looms there. She got me a rise. She got herself and me one as well ... she said we deserved one"

Norah recalls the time she decided to finish working in the mills. "I was getting on then, and I knew I shouldn't go work again ... but the boss who was over us used to bang on a can that hard it used to make me jump. When we'd bin to have a cup of tea ... you'd have so many minutes, you see ... and when it had finished ... these minutes ... he used to bang on this can and say, 'Come on ... get this work done.' So I told Arthur Goodwin I wasn't coming any more. I finished and I got a job up the Moorlands [the hospital]. I was the cleaner. I was the only domestic on the ward. It was the maternity ward ... and I stayed there about eighteen months. And then I finished work altogether." But Norah didn't finish altogether. "I washed towels and washed hair for Gwen Phillips."

Norah remembers "a spell of time when there wasn't any work ... a lot of people were out of work." She was probably thinking of the1930s. "I got a job at Churnet Works for a little while. It was dealing with material ... pulling great big pieces and rolling it up ... getting it ready for going out. I didn't stay there very long because the floor was very hot. This room that we worked in was very hot ... and my legs and feet swelled. They swelled that much I went to the doctor's ... and he said I mustn't go work ... I must stop at home. So I stayed at home for a while, but I got a job again." Moving from one mill to another and having spells of time not working was the norm for many working mothers and Norah's experience reflects this. "It's a long while when you've got children, and there was times when I'd had enough and I used to stay at home, perhaps for months, and get my house all back to normal. I could always get a job. There'd be notices outside the mills."

Norah always walked to work but remembers people coming to Leek from out of town to work. "Oh yes, people used to come ... they'd come in droves on buses. They used to all wait outside Davenport's waiting to take girls home. And when they come out of the mill at night it was like coming off a football ground ... there was that many people. It was packed ... Davenport's ... and Brough's ... all of 'em ... they was packed with people ... real busy little town Leek was. Now it's all gone ... all the lot's gone."

"I think I enjoyed working for Arthur Goodwin more than anybody. That was on that sewing machine and doing fringing and going working for him at Davenport's ... across the road. Milner's closed, and so we went ... and Arthur Goodwin went there. And he come across here for me ... see if I'd work for him. And I went on Sander and Graff across there."

Norah doesn't recall any involvement with the textile union, apart from paying some union money at Milner's. She cannot recall any incidences of strikes or disputes. "Never had anything like that when I was at work ... just glad to have a job. Everybody was in them days. Nobody had got anything. There was no money anywhere."

Interviewed, transcribed and edited by Joan Bennett

Minnie Ferguson

a report of an interview with Rowena Lovatt

Minnie Ferguson was fourteen in 1928. Her first job was as errand girl at Brough, Nicholson & Hall under Lizzie Millward. She lived in Cheddleton and she had to hand all her wages to her Mother who then gave her two shillings and sixpence (13p) for her bus fare and two shillings and sixpence pocket money. She doesn't remember how much she earned but she used to walk to work in order to save the 3d. (2p) bus fare into Leek. To check in to work she had to drop a metal disc into a box and one day she was locked out for being a few minutes late. She enjoyed being an errand girl because she could go everywhere in the factory, under Cross Street along the tunnel, or across the bridge over it. She could stop and talk to people and take her time and was always good at finding reasons for doing so! But she decided to go somewhere else for more money.

1929 saw Minnie at the Old Works, Leekbrook. Her job there was putting Pretty Polly stockings made of pure silk on to wooden boards and getting the seams in line with the edge of the board so that they were pressed correctly when she put them into the steam press. As can be imagined, these boards had to be extremely smooth so as not to snag the stockings. During the war, she worked on rayon stockings which were not fully-fashioned and didn't have seams, so getting them straight was a nightmare. The pressing room was so hot that the girls always went home wet through. Minnie enjoyed working at Leekbrook even though she was once sent home for talking too much! She didn't dare go home so she spent the afternoon walking around the mental hospital instead of facing her Mother.

When she had gone for the job her sister was already working there and the boss said, "If you're as good as her, certainly we'll have you. She's perfect". After a fortnight, he said, "You're nothing like your sister, you're always making mistakes". "Well," said Minnie, "You've got examiners, haven't you?"

On another occasion, she had been across the road to the Travellers' Rest - they went often; any excuse would do, birthdays, weddings, etc. She was locked out for being late and the boss found her outside the works and after he'd asked her why she was there he took her back inside.

Conditions were only "quite good". The toilets were outside across the yard. They were cleaned by a man who always maintained that the women's loos were worse than the men's. The canteen facilities consisted mainly of hot water to be added to the workers' own tea.

Sometimes the women were asked to go and work in the pre-boarding department. This was where the stockings were put onto steel 'legs' ready for dyeing. It was very heavy work and so when they worked there they got men's wages for doing a man's job.

There was a dispute about wages and so Minnie and her friends called in Herbert Lisle then the union secretary . He said he'd only see them in the yard. When they went out to meet him he was visible upstairs in the bosses' office, so the girls said that they would speak to him at the Foxlowe where the union had its headquarters. When that meeting took place he said, "Well, they can't pay you any more, but I'll buy you a drink". Needless to say,

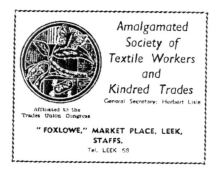

several of them stopped paying their union dues for a while.

When Minnie was still quite young she decided that she didn't want to give all her money to her Mother so she used to swap her wage slip with a girl who got less than she did and handed over the smaller amount and pay slip. When her Mother asked why the packets were open she would say, "I had to check that it was right". She had wanted the extra money because she was getting married.

Minnie remembered going on a works outing by train to Blackpool, catching the train at the Leekbrook siding. The main holiday was only a week and she spent one holiday at Penkridge. Seven of them went camping, travelling there in the back of an open top lorry with all their tents and equipment.

She left Joshua Wardles in 1950 when she went to work for Slimma when they opened their new factory in Bamgate Street. After a while, the Slimma management wanted to give the girls a shilling per week rise (5p), but they didn't get it because Herbert Lisle said that if Slimma gave it to them then all the other mills would have to pay the same, so once again the union money (6d or 3p) was withheld! She paid into the Convalescent Fund and got all the payment due to her when she was off work for six months with a bad stomach.

Her next job was at Victoria Manufacturing in Langford Street. Here, they used to put a miniature bottle of brandy into a bottle of sherry and drink it to celebrate whatever excuse they could think of. When someone had a birthday or was getting married the girls would dress them up in an outfit they had made from scraps of fabric and put them into a skip and then push them around the factory and everyone would throw rubbish at them.

Lastly she worked at Halle Models cutting trimmings, that is lace bras for nightdresses, and despite saying that she'd finish at 60 she was 66 when she finally gave up. She looks back at the old times with affection, remembering that people trusted and helped one another more in those days.

An early 1920s draft advertisement with office notes using a page from The Drapers' Organiser as a base

End Note

In 1977 Herbert Lisle, the secretary to the local textile workers' union, was interviewed for Radio Stoke and asked abut the character of Leek and how it earned its living. He considered it "a mixture of farming, textiles, Adams Butter, engineering: its quite a mixture for a small set-up," he said. "That's probably one reason why over the years the unemployment figures have been among the lowest in the country – and another reason why they don't get much assistance in the way of development grants." His experience of the town's textile manufacturing industries went back to 1946 when he moved in from Lancashire to lead the union. On his arrival he found that "the majority of firms were little family set-ups" but that recently "we've seen developments with other larger companies coming in and taking over the assets and running them successfully up to now. Take-overs have not led to any diminishing of the industry." He rather favoured the arrival of Courtaulds, for example, and gave no indication that thread and clothes manufacturing was in danger of serious decline. From the perspective of the year 2006 the picture looks very different.

One of the themes running through the life stories contained here is that of change and adaptation to new circumstances. With hindsight, individuals remember moving from job to job as though this was easy, only occasionally recalling how this was necessary because businesses stopped operating. The landscape of Leek, however, is now sharply marked by a series of mill buildings converted into apartments or retail premises. They are testimony not only to the great days of textiles in the town but also to their disappearance. A litany of former firms can be found in the memories of those who worked for them – headed by Brough, Nicholson and Hall, Wardle & Davenport, Job White, Joshua Wardle, Lux Lux, with Milners, W.H. White, Anthony Ward and Whittles close behind. The process of amalgamations and take-overs which Bert Lisle observed began with local expansions, especially that of Wardle & Davenport. This was accelerated not only by interventions by Courtaulds but also by Berisfords of Congleton, William Baird plc and Oxleys among others. In less than a quarter of a century Leek's industrial character was altered almost beyond recognition. The town started the second millennium without the mill-centred life that had dominated since the early days of Queen Victoria.

It was in this period of rapid alteration that the sixteen people who have recounted their experiences for this book worked for Leek. They remember both the way it was before the age of collapse and some aspects of the final stages in the history of the textile trades. Their testimony can be incorporated into future histories of Leek to give another dimension to the recital of take-overs, names of managing directors, sales of machinery, destructions of buildings and conversions to flats which would otherwise be the extent of the story. Not that this should be the last word. There are sections of the textile industry not represented here, dyers and office staff for example, who will have recollections well worth recording.

Working conditions and the latest technology available in the mid-1960s are well illustrated by an operator on a raschel loom (above) and the scene in a jacquard weaving room (below)